Life-Shaping Decisions

*Applying God's Word
to Career Planning*

Rick Horne

Purposeful Design Publications is the publishing division of the Association of Christian Schools International (ACSI) and is committed to the ministry of Christian school education, to enable Christian educators and schools worldwide to effectively prepare students for life. As the publisher of textbooks, trade books, and other educational resources within ACSI, Purposeful Design Publications strives to produce biblically sound materials that reflect Christian scholarship and stewardship and that address the identified needs of Christian schools around the world.

Printed in the United States of America
16 15 14 13   7 8 9 10

Horne, Rick
    Life-shaping decisions: Applying God's Word to career planning
    ISBN 978-1-58331-121-9   Student text   Catalog #7066

Purposeful Design Publications
A Division of ACSI
PO Box 65130 • Colorado Springs, CO 80962-5130
Customer Service: 800-367-0798 • www.acsi.org

Contents

Interacts

Life-Shaping Decisions

acknowledgements

This book is the result of countless hours of thoughtful input from many people. My wife and children have been my biggest cheerleaders through its writing and many rewriting stages. Betty, especially, has worked to keep my distractions to a minimum. While continuing her normally heavy family and ministry routines, when I would be home, she would answer the phone, answer the door, and settle squabbles among our six kids. She had to make a myriad of decisions that would have been more easily deferred to or discussed with me, and willingly managed our home to absorb interruptions and keep diversions away from me. Her faithfulness emerges on every page of this book. "Many women do noble things, but you surpass them all." (Proverbs 31:29)

Friends with whom I have worked for many years at the Christian Academy, especially Bob Walton, Bible department chairperson, Bob Iannacone, Paul Foster, and Dawn Bell of Delaware County Christian School, have used this material with their students and have offered invaluable suggestions. Likewise, God has used colleagues in the Christian school movement such as Dr. Ollie Gibbs, whose enthusiasm and leadership at ACSI brought this to press. Likewise, Dr. Roy Lowrie Jr., though now with the Lord, gave me years of opportunity to refine my understanding of many of the biblical concepts in this book as a faculty member of the International Institutes for Christian School Teachers and Administrators. Dr. Lowrie's manner of encouragement is impossible to ignore.

The person who has helped me the most to develop the content of this book for publisher readiness is Christian Academy graduate, doctoral candidate, teacher in higher education, and good friend Tom Wisneski. A faithful steward of the talents God has put at his disposal, Tom has spent scores of hours editing, rewriting, recommending ways the content could be better organized, and suggesting ways to shore up weak points and illustrations.

Whenever someone wants to address a topic that embraces as much of life as career planning does, there are bound to be weaknesses, underemphases, and oversights. I must take credit for these. The greatest thanks and praise, of course, for whatever helpfulness *Life-Shaping Decisions* may offer, must go to the One who has commissioned all of us to serve with the talents He's entrusted to us. May He use these few loaves and fishes to fulfill what Ezekiel repeated more than sixty times to be God's purpose: that the world "may know that I am the Lord."

Life-Shaping Decisions

introduction

Imagine yourself in a room. There are many narrow passageways that lead out from the room, but you don't know where they lead because you have never left the room. The ceiling above seems almost beyond your vision. You look this way and that, and you look up. You begin to notice that the ceiling appears clearer, more distinct than before. As time goes by, your doubts begin to fade—the ceiling is actually moving closer, gradually descending.

You have several choices: you may take any of the passageways leading out from the room; or you may stay to find out when or if the ceiling will stop descending. You step back and look up at the ceiling again. It is closer and still moving with a steady, slow descent. What will you do?

For many years now you have been in a similar situation, and only now has the ceiling begun to descend. You have been going to school, making friends, enjoying clubs or sporting activities, and going to church. All this has prepared you for the time when you need to move on. It's time to leave your room and take one of life's passageways to the future.

The future holds some uncertainty for all of us. Each of us has to choose from a different set of paths. Yet none of us has to choose a path blindly, for God has given us a guide in His Word. With its aid, we can know what certain paths promise and where they lead. If we look closely above the exits, we can make out signs: WEALTH, POWER, PLEASURE, and many others. Besides these, there is the path of FAITHFULNESS that God desires for us. Unfortunately, while it is possible for us to retrace our steps and change paths, it is rarely easy.

Bill is now 29 years old. When he graduated from high school, he "tried college" for two years and then dropped out. He worked for a nursing home as an aide for a year and a half. He went back to college for a semester, only to drop out before exams. Bill then worked part-time as a bus driver for four years. He enrolled for a semester at a trade school and left before completing a month of classes. Throughout this period of ten years, Bill also moved from church to church. Finally, he got to the point where he was willing to make some commitments about his relationship with God and about his goals for the future.

"I'm tired of bouncing," Bill confessed when looking to me for help. "No woman takes me seriously, and I don't even own a car! Eight dollars an hour looks good to someone who's been a student and has had little money for anything but the basics. Now, ten years after high school, I have nothing and I am becoming nothing. I am a disappointment to my parents and, to tell the truth, I don't even respect myself."

Jesus' description of salt that has lost its saltiness applies well to Bill's feelings about himself: "You are the salt of the earth. But if the salt loses its saltiness, how can it be made salty again? It is no longer good for anything, except to be thrown out and trampled by men." (Matthew 5:13) Bill viewed himself as "no longer good for anything, except to be thrown out." It was only through serious counseling during the next several months, and a strong commitment on Bill's part to change his priorities, that Bill began to put his life back together again.

Many teens, like Bill, make bad choices, but some never find help. Tragically, their hopes for the future are dashed. Their excitement turns to disillusion and disappointment as they pursue career plans without God's wisdom for living and working. Only a path in harmony with the principles in God's guide, His Word, will grant ultimate, lasting success.

This book is planned to help you read the Bible as your guide and apply it to your own career plans. Each chapter teaches important biblical principles for career planning. The Interact section at the end of each chapter includes a series of activities that will help you apply the principles to your own career plans. Most of the questions will require thoughtfulness and personal reflection rather than memorizing what you've read. The goal of these sections is to encourage self-awareness and practical planning for life changes that will lead to a faithful and fruitful life.

If you are using this book on your own, you may want to read parts 1, 2, and 3 before you begin to work on the Interact exercises. This first reading will give you an overall sense of what's involved in making career plans that are consistent with God's Word. After that, go back to the beginning and read each chapter while you work through the exercises in the corresponding Interact sections.

For added challenge, use the Interact exercises with a group, such as a Sunday school class, youth group, college and career group, or Christian school class. Group work can give you added perspectives about yourself and the biblical priorities you need to consider. In addition, a group can help keep you accountable to make the changes and take the steps necessary for sound career planning.

part one

**Career Stewardship and
Other Approaches to Career Planning**

You can look at the process of planning your career in a way that carries the sense of adventure you should have as you think about your future. Instead of picturing yourself in a room with a descending ceiling, see yourself at a pool with a bank of high dives. You are standing in a long line of people that stretches off into the horizon, beyond where you can see. You look at the faces of those who stand with you, and here and there you recognize people from your class or church. But you don't recognize most of these faces, though they are all about your age. The line slowly moves forward as each person eventually chooses a diving board and jumps into the water below.

As you draw closer and can see more clearly, you notice that each of the boards has a different amount of spring. You're not sure why, but most of the diving boards don't seem to work very well. Many people seem to be using them, even though the boards consistently launch them out of control, into painful belly flops or back flops. Still, there is one board that always sends its divers on graceful arcs through the air into enjoyable, refreshing splashes below.

Now it's your turn to choose which board you'll climb.

In this illustration, the diving boards represent some of the common motives that young adults have as they spring into career planning. Of the many diving boards you see stretching to the left and right, at least three stand out: wealth, interest, and fulfillment. These are the most attractive and stylish boards, so they are also the most widely advertised and the most popular. They represent three purposes that modern society wants you to adopt, and in the next four chapters we will study them closely. We'll save God's alternative, a biblically based approach to life planning (career planning affects all of life) for chapter five.

Think about your motives. As you read these pages, honestly check your career planning purposes, attitudes, and values. If you adopt the principles God has revealed in His Word, the Bible, you can pursue your career planning with confidence. You can be certain this board will spring you safely into an exciting and rewarding future. If you choose any other board, if you follow any other motive in planning your career, you can expect a disappointing and painful splash—in this life and in the one to come.

chapter one

Is Money the "Root of All Evil"?

A Defective Rudder

"Tell me what you're thinking about for next year," I asked Steve when he showed up for his senior interview.

"Memphis State, for computer science," he answered without hesitation.

"How did you come to that decision, Steve?"

"Everything I hear about the field tells me that this major and my computer science abilities will add up to some big bucks."

Steve's motives are common among thousands of his fellow students across America and the world. According to a UCLA survey of freshmen at 350 universities and colleges, new students typically say that their primary goal is to be "financially well-off." A *USA Today* poll of nearly 27,000 teens summarized their number one goal as a big "bottom line." "They pick pay over satisfaction or challenge when it comes to what they hope for in a career."

While Steve may have other motives besides wealth, his response to my question suggests that he may be heading for trouble. "Some people," Paul taught, "eager for money, have wandered from the faith and pierced themselves with many griefs." (1 Timothy 6:10b) Certainly, it is wise to consider whether you will be able to earn a living in a possible occupation. But if wealth becomes the rudder that guides your decisions, "many griefs" will await you as you set sail.

Wealth takes its toll among Christian young adults in subtle but serious ways. Sandy was a sophomore at a prestigious "Ivy League–type" Christian college. She had won an athletic scholarship that covered many of her college expenses, but it was not enough to make her acceptable to her wealthier classmates. "There was an arrogance about many people," she said. "They let me know that without preppie clothes or my own car, I wasn't all that desirable to be around. Nobody actually said this, but it was something you could feel."

After a year at a less prestigious Christian college, Sandy was convinced by the different atmosphere that wealth could have chilling effects. "My friends at the other college weren't malicious or anything. I really don't think they knew how their money affected them. The kids here seem to accept me for who I am and not because I dress right."

If wealth is a major guide in your career plans, it will have a dangerous effect on many of your other decisions too. It will affect your decisions about whether to marry and whom to marry; whether to have or not have children (and how many); where to live; whether you will give money to the church, the poor, and Christian work, and how much; how to use your leisure time; and what your political views and sense of moral justice will be. God's Word addresses each of these issues with specific moral principles, giving answers that are vastly different from those provided by an approach to life that is wealth centered.

Wealth Is Not Evil

At this point, it may be important to point out that the Bible does not condemn a person for being wealthy. Many of God's most faithful servants were wealthy: Job was "blameless and upright; he feared God and shunned evil," (Job 1:1) yet he was extremely wealthy; Abraham was wealthy too, yet the writer of Hebrews presents him as a great example of faith and obedience (Hebrews 11:8–19); David and Solomon were kings of Israel, enjoying the wealth that accompanied the position, yet David was a man after God's own heart (1 Samuel 13:14), and Solomon pleased God (1 Kings 3:10); Joseph of Arimathea, who had Christ's body placed in his own tomb, was "a rich man," yet he was a "disciple of Jesus" (Matthew 27:57) and a "good and upright man." (Luke 23:50)

Over and over Scripture makes it clear that wealth, in itself, is not evil, but the motives that people bring to wealth can be evil. "The love of money is a root of all kinds of evil. Some people, eager for money, have wandered from the faith and pierced themselves with many griefs." (1 Timothy 6:10) Here, the Apostle Paul is not criticizing the rich for having too much money or too many possessions; instead, he focuses on their motives.

It Can Distort Our Values

Still, wealth can have a destructive effect on us. It can make us partial toward those who have more than we have, critical of those who have less, and dangerously comfortable with our own position.

Shelly was planning to serve in a poor village in the Dominican Republic as part of a summer missionary team. She told one of the sponsors that she'd be taking ten different outfits for the two weeks, and she didn't know how she'd fit them all into the one suitcase she was allowed to take.

"Shelly, you'll be working alongside people from the village who will be wearing the same clothes when you begin work in the village as when you finish two weeks later."

"Ugh! How can they live like that?" she said with an air of disgust at the thought of wearing the same clothes for two weeks.

Shelly had no idea that most people in the world live very differently from us and not just because they choose to—often they have no choice. Her sponsor described the people's poor living conditions in greater detail.

"Oh," she said more meekly. "I'm just so used to the things I have. I just assumed everyone lives like I do."

To Shelly's credit, she was still willing to put herself in that very different, materially deprived situation for those two weeks—without her ten outfits. She was willing to serve those people and accept the inconveniences and discomforts out of her love for them. She opened herself up to experiences that challenged her values about wealth and that revealed her prejudices.

Most of us can think of people whose lives have been torpedoed by their desire for more and more things or money. Divorce, alcohol problems, loneliness, ulcers, heart attacks, neglected families—the list goes on. But the impact of wishy-washy or clearly materialistic values can be more subtle for young adults. The consequences of decisions shaped by these values may be delayed for a few years.

Tracie and Ned, now age 23, live with the effects of choices they made as teenagers, and they can't shake them off easily.

Ned and Tracie were high school sweethearts. They both came from professional families, and both sets of parents came from families in which they were the only college graduates. Ned's dad was an established attorney, and both of Tracie's parents were college educators. Their parents were sincerely committed Christians, but they were also firmly committed to making sure their children pursued the best colleges their academic success would allow. "After all," they reasoned, "the best way to get a good job is to go to a college with a good name." Of course, a big price tag and lots of college loans may also come with a good name.

Tracie and Ned attended two prestigious institutions, and they did well. They also became involved with InterVarsity Christian Fellowship on their respective campuses; and over time they grew in their conviction that the Lord wanted them to serve in an international missions ministry. Their earlier motivation for going to college, to get "good" jobs, was replaced by their desire to use their lives for Christ. Their love for the Lord and for each other continued to flourish in their last two years at college. They became engaged when they were seniors and were married after graduation. Now they could begin their life of service together in the mission work they'd dreamed of for the last couple of years. Right?

No. Something was wrong. They were committed Christians. They were committed to each other. They had just graduated from highly reputable universities, and they wanted to serve Christ through missions involvement with their professional talents. But they also had a combined debt of over $35,000 for their college loans. Missions would have to be put on hold.

Prestigious colleges are not necessarily wrong to attend, and it is certainly not wrong to select a college that will stretch you academically and prepare you professionally. But Tracie and Ned were set up for their disappointment and their $35,000 debt back in high school when they were seduced by the appeal of a degree from a highly acclaimed school.

Missions involvement or work in another field altogether (social work, education, business in a particular part of the country, law, etc.) may require you to accept a low salary in order to get the position you want. Ned and Tracie were seduced, in their early college planning, by thinking that security came with attending the "right" college. The way you think about wealth and the supposed security it promises can affect your future choices in serious, life-shaping ways too. You may not be able to accept a certain position, work in a situation that appeals to you, or have the flexibility you would like for marriage and family planning because of a college debt or other obligations that may come with making plans shaped by a desire for wealth. The "many griefs" that Paul talks about can take a variety of forms.

You Cannot Serve Two Masters

Either wealth can direct our career plans or God can, but they cannot be co-directors. There isn't room for both to have controlling influence in anyone's life. Christ says, "No one can serve two masters. Either he will hate the one and love the other, or he will be devoted to the one and despise the other. You cannot serve both God and money." (Matthew 6:24)

One way to test your own love of money is by examining how you handle the money that passes through your hands now. American teens have the largest amount of disposable wealth in the world. They usually don't have mortgages, insurance, or taxes to pay, so they have more money to spend as they please than any other group. One survey found that the average annual income of young people ages 15 to 19 from jobs and other sources was

$2,370 per person. How do you use the money you receive? How much do you give to the needy? How much do you use to support your church and other Christian groups? How much planning and saving do you do now for your future educational or training needs? Does the money you spend on leisure activities and luxury items satisfy God's criteria or the world's hype? (The Interact will help you think about your values in this area.)

If wealth already has a grip on you, however slight that grip may be, you must be aware of the serious impact it can have on your career planning. The world, which creates attractive illusions and promises false rewards, makes this diving board look exciting. It is crucial for you to get off this board quickly to avoid plunging into the grief and heartache that Paul warns us about in 1 Timothy 6:10.

Is Money the "Root of All Evil"?

Test yourself to see whether you have been climbing the wealth diving board.

How much does money have a grip on you? Think of the last $50 or $100 you had to spend. It may not have been a lump sum, but think of the last $50 or $100 to pass through your hands—even if it was during several weeks or months.

a. List the sources of the money and the approximate amounts.

Amount   Source

_____   _____

_____   _____

_____   _____

b. List how you used the money, and your best guess about the amount of each expenditure.

Amount   Uses

_____   _____

_____   _____

_____   _____

c. What percentage did you spend in each area? (Divide each amount spent by the total amount you had. For example: Suppose you had $50, and you spent $10 for dates; 10 divided by 50 equals .20, so you spent 20% on dates.)

Amount   Percent   How I Used It

_____   _____   _____

_____   _____   _____

_____   _____   _____

_____   _____   _____

Some ways you may have used your money include:

- Dates
- Entertainment and recreation
- Clothes that are "nicer" than necessary
- Other things that are "nicer" than necessary
- Things that are more necessary than "nice"
- Giving to your church or to another ministry

- Giving to needy people
- Savings
- Snacks
- Fast food
- Gifts for others
- Other uses

d. Compare uses of your money with the kind of spending that God urges us to do. List the uses God encourages or commands in each passage below and compare your spending with the amount you listed above.

	Areas in Which God Urges Spending	Percent I Spent
Proverbs 28:27		
Ephesians 4:28		
1 Timothy 4:4–5		
1 Timothy 5:8		
1 Timothy 5:17, 18		
1 Timothy 6:17–19		

e. Do you need to make any changes? List two good habits in your use of money that you want to continue, and two habits that you think God wants you to change:

To Continue

_____

_____

To Change

_____

_____

"Well, What Are You Interested In?"

Ed planned an engineering career right up to his high school graduation. His excellent performance in science and advanced math courses made it natural for him to follow his interest in an engineering-related field.

When Yolanda met with me in May of her junior year, she was sure she would attend the local branch of the state university to study business. One of the youth leaders in her church was a single young woman who worked as a business manager for a clothing manufacturer—a job that Yolanda thought would be very interesting.

Ed applied to a Bible college about midsummer after his graduation to train for youth ministry. A year later, after her graduation, Yolanda entered a hospital program to study radiology.

Interests Change

Ed and Yolanda illustrate what counselors typically find to be true—most young adults are either unsure of their interests or have interests that frequently change. One counselor said he finds that many juniors and seniors change their field of interest between the time he sets up an appointment to talk to them about their future plans and the actual time they meet. Sometimes only a week or two is all it takes for a change in interest to occur.

Interests, particularly in young adults, are often fickle. One university admissions counselor said that more than 25 percent of entering freshmen change their majors before they even start attending classes. "By the time they are juniors," he continued, "more than two-thirds of them change their majors two more times." Yet, "What are you interested in?" or "What would you like to do?" are the questions most often asked of young adults in their career planning.

Interests Are Unstable

Unfortunately, some school counselors encourage students to give the most serious attention to their interests when planning their futures. Although most counselors wisely direct young people to consider other factors like aptitudes and experiences, they may also, along with their parents and friends, subtly and unwisely promote interests as the most important factor for career planning.

Interest inventories and surveys may lead high school juniors and seniors to put too much confidence in their interests. In these surveys, students check tasks they "like," and then receive a list of occupations to explore, basing their choices on their survey results. Such tests may convey a misleading message: interests are the key to your future.

While interests should have a place in your career planning, they should not be your most important guide. People who try to live according to their personal interests usually have the stability and peace of "popping popcorn."

Unfortunately, confidence in personal interests is widespread. In a newspaper survey of high school seniors, 93 percent of the college-bound students and 87 percent of the not college-bound students said "interesting work" was "very important" for future satisfaction. While there is nothing wrong with "interesting work" (as we shall see), placing such importance upon interests is like playing career-planning roulette.

Israel's King Solomon, with all his wealth, power, and prestige, tried to rule his life by his interests. He freely ran from one experience to another. As soon as he got what he wanted, his interests would shift.

Later in his life he chose the word "meaningless" to describe this self-indulgent lifestyle (Ecclesiastes 1:2; 12:8). Solomon uses this word more than thirty times in the twelve brief chapters of Ecclesiastes to emphasize that living without commitment to God's mission is empty and disappointing. It is not unfilled interests but a misaligned purpose that results in "emptiness" or "meaninglessness."

You Can Cultivate Interests

Interests are like tastes for food—they change. What you once despised, you may now like; what you found appealing, you may now avoid. Often, interests are like a series of first impressions. People you don't initially appreciate may grow on you. Similarly, people in a new group who first get your attention may soon become unattractive or uninteresting. Has a teacher ever assigned a term paper topic that didn't interest you at first but became more appealing as your research progressed? Have you ever grown to like someone, perhaps even as a best friend, that you could not stand when the two of you first met?

You can develop interests in work areas as well. This is why Paul could instruct slaves, who had no freedom to choose their careers, to do their work with their whole heart, "with sincerity of heart ... like slaves of Christ ... doing the will of God from your heart. Serve wholeheartedly, as if you were serving the Lord, not men." (Ephesians 6:5–7) Although they were slaves, Paul encouraged them to serve by putting themselves fully into their work. When he said "wholeheartedly," he included their intellect and emotions, as well as their physical strength. Every area of work has unappealing and uninteresting features. Paul's command helps us understand that being enthusiastic about our work does not depend upon finding the perfect job.

The ability to work wholeheartedly comes from the inside. A job cannot produce or sustain a high level of motivation for long. At best the variety, novelty, or changing challenges of a job simply keep a role from becoming "old" and keep us thinking creatively. But even creativity can become old. Witness the depression and suicide rates among creative artists, musicians, and actors. God did not create work roles to be our primary or lasting source of satisfaction. However, the interest diving board can mislead a person to that conclusion.

Your Interests Are Still Valuable

While interests do have limitations, they can be a helpful component in your career planning. A school counselor told me several years ago that he knew a surefire way to help young people determine the will of God for themselves: "I just ask them what they want to do," he said, "and God's will for them is always the opposite." He assumed that his students were inevitably on the wrong track if they were following their own interests, even if the students were sincere and intelligent.

Such a cynical attitude denies the usefulness that interests can have in a student's career plans. Chapter 13, "Clues to Your Talents: Your Interests," will show you how to tap into them wisely. For now, it's best to see them as first impressions. They may attract you; they may catch your attention; perhaps they will motivate you to explore a certain career field more fully. But it would be foolish to base major decisions on first impressions. Impressions often change with time, and so do interests.

Your interests may offer you a good first step in some of your planning. However, the steps you take as you climb the ladder to your diving board should rest on something more stable and reliable than your interests. The challenge, in the face of great worldly pressure, is to reject such an unstable ladder. God's ladder is far more secure.

So many students are guided in their decision making by their interests. These, they are led to believe, are a sound rudder for their career-planning vessel. What do the Scriptures teach about interests? They are certainly part of our personality, but how much influence should they have in our decision making?

Read the Ephesians 6:5–8 passage and try to think about each of the questions below with these verses in mind.

1. Slaves are addressed in these verses. What are the differences in the choices that slaves and employees may have?

   _____

   _____

2. What motives did Paul urge these Christian slaves to have in their work?

   _____

   _____

3. How do these motives compare with the motives that workers commonly have today? (What are some of the most popular reasons your friends give for their career-planning choices?)

   _____

   _____

4. When Paul says "serve wholeheartedly" (v. 7), what attitudes and behaviors do you think this includes?

   _____

   _____

5. What "interest" is Paul urging as the chief motive for these workers?

   _____

   _____

6. Suppose a worker is in a job he does not like, for one reason or another, but his motives are as one "serving the Lord" (v. 7). What are three worker traits you might see him display? Why might this be true?

Trait *Example: Diligence*	Explanation *He may be conscious that he's really working for another Person, the Lord.*
a. _____	_____ _____
b. _____	_____ _____
c. _____	_____ _____

7. What are three additional traits a young woman might exhibit if her attitudes were influenced by friends and others who kept telling her, "I wouldn't put up with a job I didn't have any interest in"? *Example:* Complaining.

a. _____   b. _____   c. _____

8. Explain one way the attitudes in numbers six or seven, whether positive or negative, might affect the worker's family relationships.

_____

_____

_____

Note: This study is not intended to teach that interests are unimportant or that it is wrong to be interested in an occupational area. Chapter 13 sketches the right use of interests. These exercises are to help you put your interests into proper perspective. Interests must not be your career-planning rudder.

chapter three

A Fulfilling Career: A Goal You Can Never Attain

"Be a Girl Scout troop mother;" the radio ad concluded. "You''ll feel good about yourself if you do."

Brooke Shields, urging young people to read, says, "When I read, I know I am doing something good for myself, and I feel fulfilled. You will, too."

Feeling "good about yourself" and being "fulfilled" sound so right. It would seem unnatural for us to question these motives. Shouldn't we choose to do what will be fulfilling? We are told to pursue all sorts of causes, many of them noble, because of the personal fulfillment they offer. Unfortunately, because it is so deceptive, the diving board of fulfillment can be even more dangerous and heartbreaking than those of wealth and personal interests.

Fulfillment: A Mirage of Modern Culture

Daniel Yankelovich, a social psychologist, concluded that the shift in cultural values that started in the mid-fifties and continues today produces young people who are much more concerned with personal fulfillment than previous generations were. "My firm's studies showed more than seven out of ten Americans (72 percent) spending a great deal of time thinking about themselves and their inner lives.... The rage for self-fulfillment, our surveys indicated, has now spread to virtually the entire US population.... This premise is rarely examined, even though it leads people to defeat their own goals—and to end up isolated and anxious instead of fulfilled."[1] Ironically, by pursuing fulfillment, a person is often left terribly unfulfilled.

In interviews with people who pursued personal fulfillment, Yankelovich found disillusion and despair. Their dreams were not taking shape as they had expected. One of them confessed:

---

[1] Daniel Yankelovich, *New Rules: Searching for Self-Fulfillment in a World Turned Upside Down* (New York: Random House, 1981), 5.

When my wife told me she was going to work full-time, even though we have a three-year-old girl who needs a lot of care, I said, Sure. That's great. I get pleasure out of my work. Why should she be stuck in the house all day?

She has a right to her own fulfillment. Well, it didn't work out as well as we thought it would. The first thing we did when she went back to work was to buy a more expensive house because we had two incomes to count on. But inflation gobbled up the extra money we had from her earnings. Now we're stuck with mortgage payments at 15 percent interest. The bloom is off the rose with her job—she likes it all right but not as much as at first. We take turns caring for our little girl, so we hardly see each other; when she's home, I'm working, and vice versa. Now she can't quit the job even if she wants to; we can't afford it.[2]

Unfortunately, the modern push for self-fulfillment led this husband and wife to make choices that proved frustrating in the end. In fact, their choices brought them the very opposite of what they sought.

Students in high school are not immune to the push for fulfillment. Following her own desires and having her parents' support, Anne decided to go to an exclusive women's college. She was attracted to it because of the mystique of fulfillment and satisfaction she felt it promised her. "What I didn't realize at the time," she confided, "was that I would have to trade the standards I really believe in for a kind of pleasure and fulfillment that wouldn't last very long. What looked so good in high school was just the outside of the package. The stuff inside hurts. Is there any way I can start over?"

It's never too late to back down the ladder from a board of unwise career-planning motives. Altering your career plans won't be as easy as starting correctly would have been, but God will always prosper people of any age who adjust their purposes to please Him.

Losing Your Life to Find It

No matter how noble, neither our goals nor our jobs can give us the lasting fulfillment that Christ offers. At most, they can only delay the sense of hollowness that comes from a life apart from God.

Two thousand years ago, Jesus declared that self-fulfillment was an empty goal. He said, "Whoever finds his life will lose it, and whoever loses his life for My sake will find it." (Matthew 10:39) While "finding yourself" is not evil, making it your life's goal is evil. And, strangely, the only way for you truly to find

2
   Ibid., 19, 20.

yourself is not by aiming at what looks fulfilling but by pursuing Christ—losing your life for His sake.

In Deuteronomy 30:9–10, God promises that He will "delight in you and make you prosperous," but only if you "obey the Lord your God and keep His commands and decrees ... and turn to the Lord your God with all your heart and with all your soul." True fulfillment is a by-product of such faithfulness.

Motivations and Fulfillment

"I hate my job," George confessed. "I didn't find a job I really liked, so now I'm stuck with this one for twenty more years until I can retire. If I had to do it all over again, I'd never pick any business field. It's dog-eat-dog out there. Ulcers, high blood pressure, and a heart attack are probably all I have to look forward to. I hate my job."

The way we look at what we do can change. When George began his job eighteen years earlier, he enjoyed it a lot, but he had different motives at that time. As a Christian, he viewed his work as a mission and saw himself as one of "Christ's ambassadors" (2 Corinthians 5:20), as the "light of the world" (Matthew 5:14), as the "salt of the earth" (Matthew 5:13). But as he and his new wife began their family and purchased a home in the suburbs, his motivation for working gradually shifted. He sought to provide for more and more of the "needs" of his middle-class lifestyle, while he let his goal to serve Christ slip into the background. Slowly, unaware of what he was doing, George shifted from centering on God to centering on himself. George's exasperation stemmed not from a frustrating job in itself but from forsaking his first love, God.

Solomon had a similar sense of futility. He searched for personal fulfillment in work, education, and pleasure, but to no avail. All the occupational choices of his day were open to him, but he wasn't satisfied. "Meaningless! Meaningless!" says the Teacher. "Everything is meaningless!" (Ecclesiastes 12:8) In the end, God brought him to see that the only satisfying motive for working, learning, playing—for all his life—was to serve God. "Now all has been heard; here is the conclusion of the matter: Fear God and keep His commandments, for this is the whole duty of man." (Ecclesiastes 12:13)

Our jobs are rarely sources of lasting joy and true fulfillment. Rather, the motives with which we work are what really satisfy. For this reason, Paul gives instructions to slaves that might sound strange to a twentieth-century worker.

Slaves, obey your earthly masters with respect and fear, and with sincerity of heart, just as you would obey Christ. Obey them not only to win their favor when their eye is on you, but like slaves of Christ, doing the will of God from your heart. Serve wholeheartedly, as if you were serving the Lord, not men, because you know that the Lord will reward everyone for whatever good he does, whether he is slave or free. (Ephesians 6:5–8)

Notice how many of the phrases refer to motives. Who today would think that a slave, of all people, could find satisfaction and real fulfillment in his slavery?

By the way, Paul is not teaching people to be complacent and unwilling to improve their job status or working conditions. He teaches just the opposite in other places, as we will see later. Here, he is urging people who have almost no career choices (slaves) to engage in wholehearted—and fulfilling—service.

What is most important to you? What do you value most highly?

1. On the left, rank each factor by how important it was to you before you began doing serious thinking about your own career.

2. Then, on the right, rank each factor as you think the Master wants His stewards to value it. Note the differences if any.

Number the statements from 1 to 15: *1 = most important*; *15 = least important.*

(Note: If some of these items seem to have the same importance to you, simply give them the same number. It is possible to use the same number two or three times. Try, however, to rank as many as possible with different numbers.)

_____   a. Opportunity to help meet the needs of others   _____

_____   b. Possible earnings and fringe benefits   _____

_____   c. The will of God   _____

_____   d. Working conditions   _____

_____   e. Christian service opportunity   _____

_____   f. Retirement policy   _____

_____   g. Number of working hours   _____

_____   h. Personal interest and enjoyment   _____

_____   i. Fullest use of my talents and abilities   _____

_____   j. Opportunity for advancement   _____

_____   k. Toughness of the training requirements   _____

_____   l. Thinking about what is pleasing to God   _____

_____   m. The sense of importance that goes with the job   _____

_____   n. What my parents want me to do   _____

_____   o. How my working hours would affect my Lord's day   _____

Letters *a, c, e, i, l,* and *o* are clearly related to stewardship. The others may or may not be connected with faithful stewardship, depending on your motives and meaning for each. Which of these stewardship-related items are in your top ten? Why are they important to you?

_____

_____

_____

_____

_____

_____

_____

_____

_____

_____

From this exercise, what major change(s) do you believe you need to make if you are to spring from the diving board of faithfulness in your career planning?

_____

_____

_____

_____

_____

_____

_____

_____

_____

_____

chapter four

The "Best" Colleges—Guarantee of a Secure Future?

"I've got a 1340 on the SAT, a 3.85 GPA, and a class rank in the top ten. I think I should go to a pretty selective college. That's what employers really want to see on a résumé." Terry felt confident about his future.

Do a good job and a secure future come from getting into the right college? having the right major? interviewing with the right companies? being hired by the right firm?

To begin with, only 50 percent of college entrants will finish college. Of these, more startling yet, about a third will be under-employed, meaning that they will settle for jobs they could have had without four years of college. In other words, about 65 percent of high school grads who go to college either will not stay and graduate or will get jobs that have little to do with their college education.

Ed Herr, a Penn State University professor and an international authority on career development, says that a four-year college degree may be misleading—especially for a student in the academic middle. "The vast majority (70 percent) of high school graduates go on to college, most to four-year colleges.... Six years later, only about 50 percent actually graduate with a four-year degree. The rest 'cool out' of the higher education system, but not before most have accumulated significant financial aid debt.

"Meanwhile," Herr continues, "the employment prospects for those who do persist and obtain a four-year degree worsen. Whereas in the past, one in every five persons with a college degree failed to find commensurate employment, today it is one in three and rising."

But this does not mean that there is never any point in thinking about attending the most prestigious schools. God can use those programs, too, to further his purposes.

"Best" Isn't Necessarily an Unwise Choice

Thom had earned an academic and leadership record to appeal to admissions committees in highly selective colleges. For as long as he could remember, he had wanted to pursue a career in politics. He had committed himself to serve Christ with his life and to graduate from high school and complete a college program with a résumé that would be attractive to the world's political power brokers. He succeeded with the first part and got started on the second.

He entered Boston College's political science program. He researched the college and found that there were several strong Christian groups on campus that would support him in his Christian commitment. He discovered also that the college's political science graduates had ready access to a number of worthwhile internships. The choice he made was based on what he thought would best enable him to serve Christ with his life. The common goals of material security and the esteem of "success" were not his criteria.

Thom thought about his goals carefully, and he thoroughly researched the options he thought would help him reach them. His goals were somewhat clear, but his motives were very clear. They were centered seriously on using his life faithfully for Jesus Christ.

In the final analysis, it does not matter whether Thom pursues a political career or moves in an entirely different direction. He has positioned himself for a fruitful future. God will prosper Thom's plans, although not necessarily in the way he dreamed when he was a high school senior. But his aspirations will certainly be satisfied in terms of the more serious longings of his heart—to be used by God to make a difference in this world.

Solomon affirms that you should "commit to the Lord whatever you do, and your plans will succeed." (Proverbs 16:3) This proverb has the big picture of the Christian young adult's life in view. It is not a promise, like a blank check, to guarantee that we will reach whatever goal we plan for if we just pray the right words—even with sincerity.

It is the promise that, in light of God's eternal plan and purpose, if we commit ourselves to do His will with our ambitions and intentions, He will bring those ambitions and intentions to pass. He will make them happen. Maybe they will be the specific goals we had in mind, or maybe we'll discover that He has another more wisely designed and fruitfully productive purpose. The committed Christian cannot miss. His security does not rest on anything in this world or on any plans he can concoct. It rests on God's determined purpose to accomplish His mission in this world and to use His people with the talents they possess to do it.

Of all the young adults in the world, only Christian young adults can have the confidence that their lives mean something, and will make a difference in this world and for eternity. Their ultimate goals and plans will succeed. Such security is not guesswork or a pipe dream. It is based on God's eternal decree. Chapters 5, 6, and 18 will further address this confidence that belongs to committed Christian young adults.

Security Is Only a Way That "Seems Right"

The Bible and the daily paper alike bear testimony to the all-too-common life and career crashes of young and older adults who build their futures on achieving the "right" status or position. Nebuchadnezzar's insanity (Daniel 4), Solomon's futility (Ecclesiastes 2), the intrigue, rebellion, and assassination of many Old Testament kings (2 Kings), and the envy and bitter divisiveness spawned by the pastor Diotrephes (3 John 9, 10) make strong statements. They show that there is no guarantee of security or success just because one achieves highly or holds a certain position or status.

Security and success are never guaranteed by trusting in what is not secure. Consider how vulnerable the US and world economies are to decisions of capricious oil barons in the Middle East. Consider how unpredictable, nearsighted policies of political leaders can set up a state such as California for rolling electrical energy blackouts. Consider the fragility of technical electronics hardware that can shut down cell phones, pagers, and other telecommunications equipment because of satellite failure. Consider how many "experts" thought that whole economies, political structures, and social orders would be threatened by a technical blind spot at the turn of the century (Y2K). Consider the creation and demise of whole occupations in less than a decade. Think about those who prepared for jobs in many areas and have graduated only to find that work opportunities have shrunk and new fields for which they have no training have been born.

"There is a way that seems right to a man, but in the end it leads to death." (Proverbs 14:12) What "seems right" is not necessarily dependable. Perception is reality only in people's imaginations. One who builds his life's plan on what seems a solid foundation may well see his life become uncomfortably shaky. Inevitably, a way that only "seems right to a man" will lead to disappointment and collapse if it is not built on God's "rock" foundation of wisdom. "Best" colleges, "top-tier" colleges, and "most selective" colleges can make misleading promises to young adults. Security is not found in any of them. Instead, security is found in a relationship, not in a status, institution, or condition. "Whoever listens to me will live in safety and be at ease, without fear of harm." (Proverbs 1:33)

The Pedigree of Wisdom

History may well explain the presidential administration of William Jefferson Clinton as the folly of youth—devoid of the balance of seasoned counselors and advisers. Like Rehoboam, Solomon's heir to the throne, Mr. Clinton seemed to esteem the counsel of those of his own peer group and cultural context. Such advisers helped support what has come to be recognized as the most morally debased and ignominious administration in US history. He and his advisers led with a nearsighted here-and-now perspective on what would be wise to do or not do.

In Proverbs 8, Solomon teaches us that biblical wisdom offers counsel that has an ancient ancestry and continuing progeny. It is of a noble heritage and would be foolish to ignore.

After citing in verses 12 through 21 some of the rich fruit that wisdom grows, including the security and success borne by the "fear of the Lord," Solomon goes on to trace its pedigree.

> *The LORD brought me [wisdom] forth as the first of His works, before His deeds of old; I was appointed from eternity, from the beginning, before the world began. When there were no oceans, I was given birth, when there were no springs abounding with water; before the mountains were settled in place, before the hills, I was given birth, before He made the earth or its fields or any of the dust of the world. I was there when He set the heavens in place, when he marked out the horizon on the face of the deep, when he established the clouds above and fixed securely the fountains of the deep, when He gave the sea its boundary so the waters would not overstep His command, and when He marked out the foundations of the earth. Then I was the craftsman at His side. (Proverbs 8:22–30)*

To view all of life and to pursue all of life's goals with this "craftsman" at one's side is God's guarantee of security and success. Chapter 16 will tell you more about how to get this wisdom. The aim of this chapter, however, is to alert you to one of the most popularly appealing counterfeit sales pitches by colleges and the world at large. Getting the "best" of anything, whether college or a job offer, does not guarantee anything in God's economy. Wise planning does.

People in advertising say they are selling the "best" of something, though they often have a product that is less than the best. They hope their hype will persuade us to buy.

When you hear the "best" appeal in matters that will affect the entire direction of your life, you need to ask, "Best for what?" If the appeal of best college, for example, appears to promise success or security, you should recognize that such a guarantee is misleading at best and intentionally deceptive at worst. Either way, believing it can be self-destructive. There is fine print somewhere of which even the advertisers may be unaware. Only one foundation guarantees success:

"Therefore everyone who hears these words of mine and puts them into practice is like a wise man who built his house on the rock. The rain came down, the streams rose, and the winds blew and beat against that house; yet it did not fall, because it had its foundation on the rock. But everyone who hears these words of mine and does not put them into practice is like a foolish man who built his house on sand. The rain came down, the streams rose, and the winds blew and beat against that house, and it fell with a GREAT CRASH." (Matthew 24–27)

The security or success diving board is deceptive. "Commit to the Lord whatever you do and your plans will succeed."

Conclusion

The world offers young adults many enticing paths for their life planning. Four of the most appealing are wealth, personal interest, self-fulfillment, and the promise of security or success. Each is more subtle in its deception than the one before it. Wealth is seductive, and "whoever loves wealth is never satisfied." (Ecclesiastes 5:10) Our interests fascinate us, but they change so often that to follow them is like chasing after the wind. Self-fulfillment and finding oneself appear to be noble pursuits, but they only lead to the tragedy of losing oneself. Security or success based on the common promises of our culture will prove hollow and elusive. Only when we put God at the center of our search can we discover who we really are. The next chapter will take a look at an altogether different path: one that offers true wealth, stimulates our interests, and provides genuine fulfillment and security God's way.

(A study to use as part of your devotions)

The book of Proverbs refers to many temporal (in this life) outcomes of living life either from God's perspective or from a human perspective. A God-perspective is referred to as having the "fear of the Lord." (Proverbs 1:7; 8:13; 9:10) The alternative is living in the fear of people—wanting human approval, depending on human wisdom, and pursuing goals popular with humans. (Proverbs 29:25)

The 31 chapters of Proverbs contain almost 700 positive and negative references to temporal outcomes. All of these outcomes, positive for the wise and negative for the foolish, will be fully experienced in eternity. God's providence, however, often does allow people to experience generous degrees of His goodness or the consequences of their self-destructive behavior in this life as well. But the fullness of these outcomes is yet to come.

1. For each part of Proverbs referenced below, list the features of security or success that ultimately come to one who fears the Lord and the features of insecurity or failure that come to one who does not. Keep in mind God's eternal timetable for the fulfillment of these outcomes. Their fulfillment is certain, but it will not be according to our calendar.

Features of success/security connected with the fear of the Lord	Features of success/security connected with attitudes other than the fear of the Lord
Proverbs 3	Proverbs 3
1.	1.
2.	2.
3.	3.
4.	4.
5.	5.
6.	6.
7.	7.
8.	8.
9.	9.
10.	10.

Features of success/security connected with the fear of the Lord	Features of success/security connected with attitudes other than the fear of the Lord
Proverbs 8	Proverbs 8
1.	1.
2.	2.
3.	3.
4.	4.
5.	5.
6.	6.
7.	7.
Proverbs 9:1–6	Proverbs 9:13–18
1.	
2.	
3.	
4.	
5.	
6.	
7.	

2. As you watch television, keep a pad and pencil handy. List some commercials that appear to promise security or success to those who use certain products.

Advertisement/product	How ad seems to promise success or security
1.	1.
2.	2.
3.	3.
4.	4.
5.	5.

chapter five

Career Stewardship: The Only Board for a Confident Dive

Again, [the kingdom of heaven] will be like a man going on a journey, who called his servants and entrusted his property to them. To one he gave five talents of money, to another two talents, and to another one talent, each according to his ability. Then he went on his journey. The man who had received the five talents went at once and put his money to work and gained five more. So also, the one with the two talents gained two more. But the man who had received the one talent went off, dug a hole in the ground and hid his master's money.

After a long time the master of those servants returned and settled accounts with them. The man who had received the five talents brought the other five. "Master," he said, "you entrusted me with five talents. See, I have gained five more."

His master replied, "Well done, good and faithful servant! You have been faithful with a few things; I will put you in charge of many things. Come and share your master's happiness!"

The man with the two talents also came. "Master," he said, "you entrusted me with two talents; see, I have gained two more."

His master replied, "Well done, good and faithful servant! You have been faithful with a few things; I will put you in charge of many things. Come and share your master's happiness!"

Then the man who had received the one talent came. "Master," he said, "I knew that you are a hard man, harvesting where you have not sown and gathering where you have not scattered seed. So I was afraid and went out and hid your talent in the ground. See, here is what belongs to you."

His master replied, "You wicked, lazy servant! So you knew that I harvest where I have not sown and gather where I have not scattered seed? Well then, you should have put my money on deposit with the bankers, so that when I returned I would have received it back with interest.

"Take the talent from him and give it to the one who has the ten talents. For everyone who has will be given more, and he will have an abundance. Whoever does not have, even what he has will be taken from him. And throw that worthless servant outside, into the darkness, where there will be weeping and gnashing of teeth." (Matthew 25:14–30)

Jesus used the parable of the talents to illustrate the principle of stewardship, a principle that must be central in our career planning. Too often we limit the application of the stewardship principle to how we handle our money, an understandable mistake since money is a key element in the parable. But Jesus is showing that stewards must give an account for all their life-shaping decisions, including their career plans.

Two Kinds of Stewards

In Jesus' day, a steward was a slave with special responsibilities, like those of a manager. Because his master trusted him, the steward was put in charge of his master's wealth, property, and many household decisions. Joseph's role in Potiphar's household illustrates the steward's role (Genesis 39). Potiphar, an Egyptian official, placed all the affairs and decisions of his household at Joseph's disposal. He put Joseph "in charge of his household and of all that he owned.... With Joseph in charge, he did not concern himself with anything except the food he ate." (Genesis 39:5, 6)

The stewards in the parable of the talents perform a function that is similar to Joseph's. The master entrusts each with a share of his estate. He gives one steward five talents (a talent was more than a thousand dollars in today's money); he gives another steward two talents; and he gives a third steward one talent. The first two stewards invest their master's money while he is away, but the third buries his talent.

When the master returns, he examines his servants' activities and rewards them accordingly. He commends the first two for their faithful investments, and he condemns the third for his wickedness and laziness. For the first two, the master uses exactly the same words of praise, "Well done, good and faithful servant!" They have taken the wealth entrusted to them and used it wisely, according to their master's wishes. As a result, the master rewards them with greater privilege, authority, and responsibility: "You have been faithful with a few things; I will put you in charge of many things. Come and share your master's happiness!" Although they are given different amounts of wealth, they both enjoy the master's blessing because both are faithful and wise.

The third steward is not faithful. He is not wise, for he buries his talent. On top of this, he refuses to accept any blame but Instead finds fault with the master's character ("I knew that you were a hard man") and claims to have emotional problems ("I was afraid"). The master sees through these excuses and recognizes the servant for what he is: "You wicked and lazy servant!" The servant's problem is not that he is paralyzed by fear of a hard taskmaster, but that he is self-indulgent and lazy. Perhaps the servant is pursuing wealth, or his own personal interests, seeking fulfillment or looking for a secure investment opportunity. Certainly, he is not interested in his master's will and does not consider the master's purposes as he makes his plans. Thus he lives in a way that he finds appealing, and he buries his master's wealth.

Loss and Privilege

The third steward is a warning to all of us. If we adopt his way of living, we can expect the same tragic results. At his master's command, the man who lives to please himself is stripped of all that he has and is thrown "outside, into the darkness, where there is weeping and gnashing of teeth."

The self-centered servant gives us a warning to heed, but Jesus also uses the parable for our encouragement. Some stewards squander what they have, but others invest their resources wisely. Their outcomes differ greatly: "For everyone who has will be given more, and he will have an abundance. Whoever does not have, even what he has will be taken away from him." While unfaithfulness results in judgment and exile, faithfulness yields greater privilege and blessing. We can see real-life results of these two ways of living in the way some workers' opportunities for advancement increase or decrease, depending on their faithfulness. We'll have more to say about this later.

Created to Serve

From the very beginning, God created men and women to be worker-stewards. Work was not part of God's curse upon fallen humans. God placed Adam in the garden, before he sinned, "to work it and take care of it." (Genesis 2:15) Only as a result of Adam and Eve's sin did God curse humanity's work with toil, pain, and sorrow. (Genesis 3:17–19) Only with the Fall did our attitudes toward our work change from joy and gratitude to spite and complaint.

Our motives shifted too, from God-centered to self-centered. Paul urges us to return to the motives for which we were created, to reject the sinful and distorted motives that we come by naturally, and to exhibit the purer motives of a follower of Christ—wise and faithful stewardship. "Serve wholeheartedly, as if you were serving the Lord." Real and lasting occupational fulfillment depends on whether or not we view our work as service to God.

It isn't wrong for us to select occupations that we expect to enjoy. All of us are different, and we all like some kinds of work better than others. But our general satisfaction, fulfillment, and enjoyment in work are not bound by the kind of jobs we have any more than they were for the slaves that Paul admonished to "serve wholeheartedly." (Ephesians 6:7) What matters most is our commitment to be faithful and wise stewards for our Master.

The master in the parable said to the two faithful stewards, "Come and share your master's happiness." (Matthew 25:21) While it is not unspiritual to be happy in our work, we have been created not to find true happiness by seeking it directly but by seeking first to serve our Master. Job satisfaction is a by-product of faithful stewardship, and at the core of it is our relationship with God.

Faithful Stewardship Involves All of You

You may be tempted to view your spiritual life as just one of many compartments in your life. You have many interests, and your relationship with God is just one of them. You may try to justify separating your career plans from your relationship with God, but you are only setting up a false (and dangerous) division. You should consider your career plans, like every aspect of your life, within the framework of your relationship with God. It is impossible to serve God in your spiritual life and also to serve money, or personal fulfillment, or anything else in your career planning. To be a Christian and to love God is to seek to serve Him wholly, with every part of your being, with all your motivations, aspirations, and actions. "No one can serve two masters. Either he will hate the one and love the other, or he will be devoted to the one and despise the other. You cannot serve both God and money." (Matthew 6:24)

A rabbi asked Jesus, "Of all the commandments, which is the most important?" "The most important one," answered Jesus, "is this: 'Hear, 0 Israel, the Lord our God, the Lord is one. Love the Lord your God with all your heart and with all your soul and with all your mind and with all your strength.'" (Mark 12:28–30) Jesus leaves no room for divided loyalties.

Whether you are a Christian or not, you are a steward. God has given talents to all of us, and we have a set time for investing that wealth before we are called to give an account. If you are a Christian, your genuine faith leads you to want to live to please your Lord. (Romans 6:22; 8:13, 14; 1 John 3:3) You will receive His approval and hear the words, "Well done!"

If you are not serious about following Christ, however, you are living to pursue your own purposes. You may hope to please God by showing kindness to others, but your hopes will be tragically disappointed because you are still living by your own agenda, not the Master's. The very good you hope to be doing is at best helping people live more comfortably the way they are—without Christ. Such living is shortsighted. Until we recognize that we are unfaithful and self-centered stewards by nature, and commit our lives to Jesus Christ as our Lord and Savior, we will be unable to please our Master. (Romans 8:8; 1 Corinthians 2:14)

Christian young adult, you "are God's workmanship, created *in Christ Jesus* to do good works, which God prepared in advance for us to do." (Ephesians 2:10) The Christian is God's workmanship, His project. He or she is fashioned according to God's eternal purpose, to do His work, "which God *prepared in advance* for us to do." Believers have this purposeful identity. They are *in Christ Jesus*.

Young adult decision-maker, how are you spending the valuable talents that God has entrusted to you? What are you pursuing? What diving board are you mounting? What path are you taking?

If you are serious about your career plans, and if you want to make wise decisions about your future, the only suitable path is that of faithful and wise stewardship. All other paths end in regret and tragedy. You must come to see your career plans as part of your stewardship to God. Entrust yourself to the Master, Jesus Christ. Present yourself in free and complete submission to His wise, loving Lordship. Enjoy the delights and refreshment that come from "losing your life" for His sake. (Matthew 10:39)

1. What does wise and faithful stewardship look like in real life?

    a. Read Genesis 39—the story of Joseph in Potiphar's household and as chief prison attendant. List the character qualities, skills, and abilities that Joseph must have possessed that made him a faithful and wise steward in his master's judgment, and later in that of the prison official.

    In Potiphar's house

    _____

    _____

    _____

    In prison

    _____

    _____

    _____

    b. If these incidents in Joseph's life show him to be a wise and faithful steward, what relationship is there between my being in the occupation of my choice and my being a wise and faithful steward? Is the one dependent on the other? Explain.

    _____

    _____

    _____

    c. If circumstances do not determine the quality of stewardship, what does?

    _____

    _____

    _____

2. The unjust steward was not the first to use excuses like "I was afraid." God rejected Moses' excuses 1,400 years earlier just as He rejected the excuses of the steward Jesus told about.

    a. Read the story of Moses in Exodus 3:1–4:17 and summarize each of Moses' four excuses.

Excuse 1 (3:11)

_____

_____

_____

_____

Excuse 2 (3:13)

_____

_____

_____

_____

Excuse 3 (4:1)

_____

_____

_____

_____

Excuse 4 (4:10)

_____

_____

_____

_____

b. What would Moses' excuses sound like today if a young person used them to avoid investing his talents as God urged him to? Write a modern version of each of his excuses.

Excuse 1 (3:11)

_____

_____

_____

_____

Excuse 2 (3:13)

_____

_____

_____

_____

Excuse 3 (4:1)

_____

_____

_____

_____

Excuse 4 (4:10)

_____

_____

_____

_____

part two

Your Talents and Your Career Plan

So far, we have been able to distinguish several poor alternatives and one wise one among the diving boards that you can climb. We have seen that the diving board of career stewardship is the only one that can guarantee a safe and enjoyable future. But the question remains, How do we climb that high dive? What do we need to know about ourselves to make wise life-shaping decisions? What should we take into consideration as we seek to please God and be honorable stewards? The answer lies in our talents.

Chapters 6 through 14 focus on talents. We begin by defining talents. Then we sketch a variety of those God indicates all of us have to some degree. The Interacts will help you assess your own experience in each of those talent areas. You may want to think of those talents as steps that you must carefully consider as you climb the ladder to God's diving board of career stewardship.

chapter six

Talents: What Are They?

Tim flopped into the chair in my guidance office. He is six feet three inches tall, seventeen years old, a senior who has scored more than 1,000 points in his high school basketball career, and was the all-conference MVP for two years running.

"Basketball is all I know. I can't do anything else, and yet I'm not good enough for any top college team. I don't know what to do about next year." Tim feels he has only one talent, and that one is useless.

Ann has been selected for district, regional, and state chorus from among thousands of public and private school competitors. Her soprano performances have won her wide recognition and a $2,000-a-year scholarship for four years as a voice major at a Christian college. She is confident about her next step; her talents and her plans for the future seem obvious.

Andrew gets average grades and plays intramural sports. During his high school years, he won no elections, received no awards. "I've been thinking that maybe I'll just try to get a job after graduation," he says. Andrew feels talentless.

"Everyone says I'm attractive and talented, but I'm totally confused. I have no idea what I should do after graduation." Cecilia was not exaggerating others' opinions. She is graduating as valedictorian, and she is a National Merit finalist with SAT scores over 1,400. Colleges have offered her academic and athletic scholarships. She feels too talented.

Tammy wants to "just get married and have kids." The idea of finding and using her talents seems too complicated to her. "I've loved kids for as long as I can remember. I believe that's right for me." Tammy is not even thinking about her talents.

Where do you fit in? Are you aware of your talents, or are you, like Tammy and many others, confused about what your talents might be and how to use them? Maybe you feel you don't have any, or maybe you are one of those rare persons who have identified their talents and know how they will use them.

Talents and "Talentwarp"

These students are all looking at a dark horizon in their lives. To some of them, the sun is about to rise; to others, its last traces are disappearing. Each interprets the signs on the horizon differently. Tim is depressed by what he sees, Andrew feels hopeless, and Cecilia is confused. Tammy thinks she can avoid what's coming, and Ann thinks she can sail off with ease into a new dawn. All five of them suffer from a common and disorienting condition known as "talentwarp." Talentwarp is the destructive idea that talents are limited to extraordinary skills and abilities. By thinking about talents in this way, they have narrowly restricted the way they think about their futures. Likewise, talentwarp can distort our vision and hinder our career planning.

Far from being limited to just extraordinary abilities and skills, your talents include everything that enables you to serve God and others, the entire spectrum of your unique personal resources. These include your personality, your abilities and skills, your gender, your spiritual gifts, your race, and even your socioeconomic class. As a steward, you are accountable for every aspect of your life. Each of your distinct qualities is a part of the portfolio of talents that God has entrusted to you. Each quality equips you to fulfill the unique purposes He has for you.

In fact, most occupations draw on these kinds of wide-ranging talents, rather than on outstanding or unusual abilities. Every year, graduates who receive a broad liberal arts education are hired for managerial, technical, or professional positions for which they have had no specific training. (Liberal arts is a general field including a range of subjects such as literature, history, math, and psychology.) In comparison, the number of people whose jobs require extraordinary abilities—such as professional musicians, artists, and athletes—is only a tiny fraction of the entire job market. Most careers do not require specific, outstanding abilities, but general strengths that draw on the wide spectrum of our individual talents.

If you suffer from the classic symptoms of confusion about your talents, you may have talentwarp. The antidote is an accurate, biblical understanding of talents.

Your Talents Are Unique

You are a one-of-a-kind creation; there are no duplicates or copies, no second printings. Like the stewards in the parable, you are a unique individual to whom God has given special talents to invest for Him.

Also, like the stewards who were not responsible for each other's investments, you are not accountable for investing talents you don't have. The master did not judge the unfaithful steward for having fewer talents than the other stewards, but for misusing the talent he had. Each of us will also face the Master separately, as in the parable, and be judged according to how well we invest our own unique array of talents. He has given us all different talents, "each according to his ability," and He will examine us with our individuality in mind.

Christians are God's "projects-in-progress." The Apostle Paul asserts that we are "God's workmanship, created in Christ Jesus to do good works." (Ephesians 2:10) Moreover, God's plans for us are not last-minute improvisations; they are not accidental. The "good works" planned for us were "prepared in advance for us to do." God fitted us with specific talents so we may faithfully and wisely fulfill His purposes. We are saved to serve. Because of our unique and privileged endowment, we can look to the future with confidence, knowing that God has something special in mind for each of us.

Those who do not know Jesus cannot claim this confidence. While God has generously provided them with talents, they exploit their gifts for self-centered purposes, like the "wicked and lazy" steward. In Romans 2:5–6, Paul describes the bleak future awaiting such unfaithful stewards: "But because of your stubbornness and your unrepentant heart, you are storing up wrath against yourself for the day of God's wrath, when His righteous judgment will be revealed. God will give to each person according to what he has done." Paul pictures people making deposits of wrath for themselves in the bank of God's judgment. Instead of investing their talents for God's glory, they spend it for their own, thus building up an account of future sorrow.

God's Economy: Use It or Lose It

Your unique talents never remain the same. The master said, "You have been faithful with a few things; I will put you in charge of many things," and "everyone who has will be given more, and he will have an abundance." In a different context, Jesus said, "Whoever has will be given more, and he will have an abundance. Whoever does not have, even what he has will be taken from him." (Matthew 13:12)

Your career stewardship is an ongoing process. If you seek to use all your talents faithfully and wisely, God will prosper your efforts and grant further opportunity for service. If, on the other hand, you are neglectful and unfaithful, God will withdraw His blessing. Many people use their talents to achieve fame, accumulate wealth, and earn a reputation as a successful professional. Yet, all the while, as they use their talents for their own purposes, they slowly lose the opportunity to build up lasting and eternal wealth—they fail to use their talents for God. "Do not store up for yourselves treasures on earth, where moth and rust destroy, and where thieves break in and steal. But store up for yourselves treasures in heaven, where moth and rust do not destroy, and where thieves do not break in and steal." (Matthew 6:19–20)

Steve was just about to graduate from high school, and he did not know what to do with his life. He often reviewed the Romans 12:1and 2 teaching about presenting his body to the Lord as a "living sacrifice." But he still couldn't make any confident, long-range plans about his future. He decided to attend a Bible college for a year or so, figuring that the training would be useful later, regardless of his eventual career. He also thought the time might help him to mature and reflect on how he could wisely and faithfully serve God.

While he was in high school, Steve had worked with younger children and had some opportunities to exercise leadership among his peers. As his first year at college progressed, he began to sense how useful this background was: he was able to lead Bible studies, help with his church's youth group, and talk with some of his college friends about their personal problems. He began to think seriously about some kind of career that would involve working with young people.

Steve decided to continue at the college and later at a university. He now teaches astronomy in a public high school and at a nearby college. He has written one astronomy textbook and has been increasingly active in his local church. Steve's influence and ministry expanded year by year as he held onto his original motivation to invest himself for the Lord.

A dozen or more years ago, Steve had no idea that this would be his career path. Though he was unsure of his future, he was faithful to God, and God blessed him. "Commit to the Lord whatever you do, and your plans will succeed." (Proverbs 16:3) God developed and expanded Steve's opportunities beyond his ability to plan for them. While he did not know in detail what the future would bring his way, he had the assurance that faithfulness to God would result in greater opportunity in the future.

Frank's case was more tragic. At 18, he entered a state university and immediately became involved with InterVarsity, a Christian ministry on non-Christian college campuses. For three years, he participated in college outreach. He led some of the campus meetings and shared his faith with non-Christians.

Frank was well-liked and had average grades, but he was lazy. He tended to settle for whatever came his way. He went to college because most of his friends went, and his parents said they would help pay his way. He was a communications major because that field seemed interesting. He had no goals for the rest of his life, nor was he concerned.

After his junior year, Frank quit college. He got a job as an insurance sales trainee but left after eight months. To fill his time and pay his bills, he got two part-time jobs in a shopping mall and a pizzeria. He did his work well and people liked him, but he never showed any initiative.

Meanwhile, when his parents urged him to get involved at church, Frank started teaching a sixth-grade Sunday school class. That was six years ago. His pattern of job instability and aimlessness have lost him the respect of adults and teens. Now, at age 27, Frank receives little encouragement from any his elders to engage in public Christian service. Frank is depressed. He would like to marry, and he can't understand why none of the young single women at church will date him seriously.

Throughout this period, Frank has given little thought to his accountability to God. Though he does not live in a blatantly immoral, godless way, his opportunities for service have steadily shrunk, illustrating one of the principles of God's talent economy: if you neglect to invest your talents faithfully for the Lord, you lose opportunities to serve Him. Use it or lose it. You never stay the same.

Complete Investment

God outfits each of us with a wide-ranging set of talents. To serve Him best, we need to draw on this complete array and invest it completely. To focus only on intellectual or athletic abilities, for instance, is to make an incomplete investment. Paul commands us to make a total commitment: "offer your bodies as living sacrifices, holy and pleasing to God." (Romans 12:1) Peter urges the same radical devotion: "Each one should use whatever gift he has received to serve others, faithfully administering God's grace in its various forms." (1 Peter 4:10) Be "living sacrifices" and "use whatever" you have received. This is the language of total commitment.

As noted in the previous chapter, Jesus leaves no room for divided loyalties. Likewise, He condemns divided investments. No matter what its direction, a four-cylinder car does not run well, if at all, on two or three cylinders. All four cylinders must run properly if the car is to achieve maximum performance. The Christian, too, cannot expect to find God's blessing if she serves God half-heartedly, neglecting the full range of her talents. We must commit ourselves exclusively—and fully—to God.

1. How does a distorted view of talents affect a young person's attitude toward career planning?

    a. Reread the first six paragraphs of chapter 6 and summarize Tim's, Ann's, Andrew's, Cecilia's, and Tammy's feelings about their futures because of their distorted views of their talents.

Tim's feelings about the future:

_____

_____

_____

_____

Ann's feelings about the future:

_____

_____

_____

_____

Andrew's feelings about the future:

_____

_____

_____

_____

Cecilia's feelings about the future:

_____

_____

_____

_____

Tammy's feelings about the future:

_____

_____

_____

    b. If each of these students had an accurate view of what talents are, even though their under-standing of themselves was limited, how might their feelings about the future differ from those you sketched above?

Tim's more accurate view of the future:

_____

_____

_____

Ann's more accurate view of the future:

_____

_____

_____

Andrew's more accurate view of the future:

_____

_____

_____

Cecilia's more accurate view of the future:

_____

_____

_____

Tammy's more accurate view of the future:

_____

_____

_____

_____

2. Two truths that the parable of the talents teaches are that *talents are fitted to each of us uniquely* and that *we either use or lose our talents*.

Read the passage listed beside each of the people below and put a check mark in the space to the right of each, showing which truth is illustrated most in his or her life.

Person	Passage	Talents Fit	Use or Lose
Saul	1 Samuel 13, 15		
Ruth	Ruth 3, 4:13–22		
David	1 Samuel 17		
Abigail	1 Samuel 25		
Moses	Exodus 3:1–4:17		
Ehud	Judges 3:12–30		
Nehemiah	Nehemiah 1:11b–2:1		
Esther	Esther 3, 4		
Haman	Esther 7		
Daniel	Daniel 1		
Amos	Amos 7:14, 15		
Jonah	Jonah 1, 3		

chapter seven

How to Avoid Career-Planning Fantasy or Despair

Talentwarp, the destructive condition that stems from defining talents too narrowly as spectacular abilities, often has either of two career-crippling side effects: fantasy or despair. *Career-planning fantasy* occurs when we overestimate our talents. *Despair* takes its toll on our career plans when we underestimate our talents. Fantasy is unrealistically optimistic, and despair is unrealistically pessimistic. God's perspective helps us strike a balance by teaching us to think of talents more broadly and realistically.

Career-Planning Fantasy

Earl was a D and C student throughout his entire high school career, and when he took his PSAT in his junior year, he scored among the lowest quarter of his peers. He never played sports for his school, did anything with his class, or participated in any extracurricular activities. His job and his car were all he cared about. In March of his senior year, he filled out a high school evaluation form. His remarks revealed anger, bitterness, and frustration: "If I had been given the courses I needed, I could be a doctor. I've always wanted to go to medical school, but your school has ruined my future."

Earl was pursuing a career-planning fantasy based on unrealistic expectations about his abilities. His test scores, grades, and college boards were so far below average that it was unlikely any college would accept him as a premed, biology, or science major. If Earl continued this fictional view of himself, he was headed for lifelong discouragement, frustration, and anger. Whether at college or on the job, Earl would be evaluated according to his real talents, not the talents he imagined he had. Reality would meet him face to face, no matter how high his expectations.

When you tell people your plans, do they react with a look that says, "she's living in a dream world" or "this guy is crazy"? While there is a place for dreaming and hoping about career possibilities, your dreams and hopes must correspond with the real talents that God has given you.

America is a land of vast occupational opportunities, but they don't all fit you. A well-meaning friend, even a parent, may encourage you to "be anything you want to be," but you'll need to be more realistic. If you want to avoid career-planning fantasy, you will need to recognize your limitations. While there are more than 20,000 different job titles in the *Dictionary of Occupational Titles*, many of them require specific training that you may not be able to receive because of academic, financial, or other limitations. Our limitations restrict our range of plausible choices, but our talents ensure that we will have choices.

Moreover, the Master has given you specific talents that you are to invest to the best of your ability. Therefore, you should give most of your attention to those occupations that take full advantage of who you are, those in which you can best serve God with the widest range of talents He has given you. What matters most is that we wisely and faithfully invest our real talents among the many alternatives that our modern world of work presents.

Career-Planning Despair

For teenagers, despair about career plans is often linked to despair about life in general. One psychologist in a Los Angeles suicide prevention center said, "Suicidal adolescents suffer from tunnel vision: an inability to be objective about their problems. They feel hopeless, helpless, and hapless because of what they do or do not see." It is this hopelessness, this despair about the future, that often frustrates young adults. They see nothing remarkable about themselves, so they doubt their usefulness. They look to the future, and instead of opportunities they see roadblocks.

This sort of despair often begins when young people believe what others say about them: "You'll never amount to anything!" an angry father or teacher says. "No college will ever look at you with these grades." "And besides that, your room looks like a pigsty," Mom adds. "If you don't straighten out, you'll probably drop out of school and amount to nothing!"

In addition to enduring such put-downs, young adults may be rejected by their peers, excluded from popular cliques, and generally treated as losers. Slowly they develop tunnel vision about their potential usefulness. Perhaps they have heard such messages throughout their elementary and junior high years, and by their senior year they may have little motivation to make plans for the future: "There's no point to it. I can't do anything anyway."

This may be an extreme example, but if your tendency is to be down on yourself, to feel hopeless or discouraged about your future, you are in danger of succumbing to career-planning despair. What you need is a healthy dose of honesty about yourself as God sees you.

Think of Yourself Accurately

You have been created as a unique person with definite abilities and skills that enable you to serve God in a special way. If you appraise yourself accurately, you will find many qualities that mark you as a steward who has the potential, and whom God intends, to be very useful. Each of us has been created in the image of God. Though that image has been marred by our inherited (original) sin and our present sins, we cannot completely erase our divine likeness. God has chosen to use imperfect ambassadors and managers to carry out His purposes. A broad view of your talents, beyond the narrow view of outstanding abilities, will help you to be right-minded and to avoid the despair or discouragement that can sap initiative and enthusiasm from your career planning.

When people with these two views approach their futures, they react in almost exactly opposite ways. As the ceiling gradually descends in that room, despairing individuals look from path to path and may eventually decide to make no plans to leave the room. Their downcast spirit may cause them to procrastinate or to drag themselves sluggishly along one of the paths, and all because they misread their abilities. It is as if they were committing a kind of career-planning suicide.

On the other hand, dreamers overestimate their abilities. As the ceiling descends, they casually look over their options, refuse to examine themselves closely, and recklessly run down a path in pursuit of their career-planning fantasies.

The paths start in opposite directions, but they end at the same place—ruin. You need an honest view of your talents and a practical idea about how to develop them and where to invest them. Romans 12:3 encourages this realistic self-scrutiny: "Do not think of yourself more highly than you ought, but rather think of yourself with sober judgment…."

Solomon urged workers of his day to take a careful, accurate inventory of their resources as a prelude to a wise and faithful use of them. His words apply to every young adult who wants to be a faithful steward with his or her talents:

> *Be sure you know the condition of your flocks, give careful attention to your herds; for riches do not endure forever, and a crown is not secure for all generations. When the hay is removed and new growth appears and the grass from the hills is gathered in, the lambs will provide you with clothing, and the goats with the price of a field. You will have plenty of goats' milk to feed you and your family and to nourish your servant girls. (Proverbs 27:23–27)*

The next seven chapters will help you to "know the condition of your flocks"—that is, to gain a healthy understanding of your talents and to construct a solid foundation for your career planning.

How to Avoid Career-Planning Fantasy or Despair

Orientation to Your Career Stewardship Profile (CSP).

In the next seven chapters and Interacts, you will be looking closely at your talents. If you interpret yourself accurately, you will not experience career-planning fantasy or despair. These exercises are to help you think about yourself accurately.

To help you to keep a broad and accurate view of your talents in mind, you will be guided step-by-step in completing your personal Career Stewardship Profile (CSP), which is on page 174. Fill in your CSP as you complete the exercises in Interacts 8–14. The sample CSP that follows will suggest the kinds of information you can identify and use to complete your own CSP.

Your CSP will not give you a magic formula for future planning, but it will give you a practical way to think about who God has made you along with important information for putting together a specific post–high school plan. Chapter 21, "Turn Your Findings Into aWise, Life-Shaping College Decision," will get you started in your exploration process. Your thoughtfulness with Life-shaping Decisions will add depth and wisdom to your planning. Use the book *Walking Through the College Planning Process* (ACSI, 2001) to develop a practical plan that will help you to be faithful with the talents the Lord-has entrusted to you. First, notice that the CSP is divided into three broad segments: the "Personal Growth Area," the "Professional Growth Area," and the "General Kinds of Programs."

Career Stewardship Profile

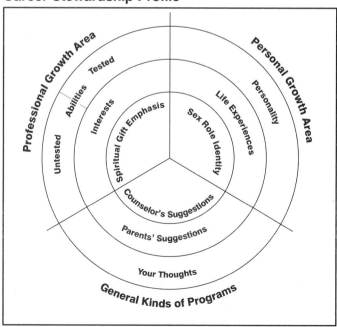

The two upper segments include talents that relate to your personal and professional planning. Some talents—abilities, interests, and spiritual gifts—seem to be related to the professional sphere. This is because we usually refer to these first when making occupational choices or further educational plans. Other talents—experiences, sex role identity, and personality qualities—seem to fit easily into the personal segment. While this division is convenient for our thinking and planning, it is an artificial division. In reality, all of your life will be affected by talents in both the personal and professional segments.

Finally, the third segment of the CSP will give you a place to summarize programs that your counselor or adviser, your parents, and you think may be wisest for you to consider to help you develop your unique talents.

Ask yourself, What programs will best support me to be the whole person God has created me to be?

Jeff's completed Career Stewardship Profile shows how his thinking progressed as he worked with the Interact exercises of each unit.

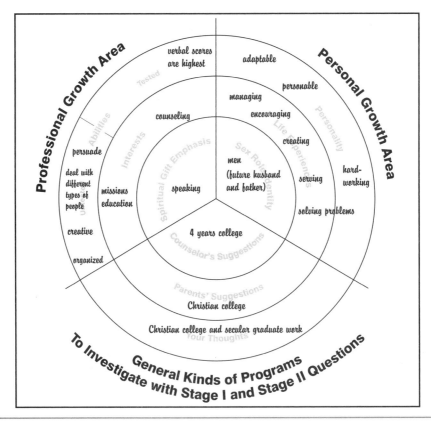

chapter eight

Clues to Your Talents: Your Personality

Take a minute to think about this: Who are or have been the primary influ-
ences in your life, and why? Is it their special abilities that make them so important to you? Or is it their personality qualities?[1] Typically, the individuals
who most influence our lives are not people who have outstanding abilities
but people (adults or peers) who have shown us kindness when we were
grumpy, patience when we were rash and impetuous, gentleness when we
were spiteful, understanding and sensitivity when we were hurt. They have
offered us wisdom when we were confused and encouragement when we
were ready to give up. Their skills may have been helpful, but their personality qualities have probably made the greatest impact. The unique character-
istics of your personality, too, even more than your special skills, will
determine how well you can fulfill God's purposes.

The Influence of an "Uncool," Caring Person

Sarah is not pretty. She may not even have average looks. She came to our
school in ninth grade. Her family was lower middle class, largely because
her father was ill and unable to work. Sarah grew up caring for him until he
died when she was fifteen. She made his meals, cleaned up for him, and
even helped him dress while her mom worked in a local food market.

I met Sarah in the middle of her freshman year after a home economics
teacher asked me to attend a meeting she was having with Sarah's mother.
The teacher wanted to talk about Sarah's personal hygiene. Sarah smelled,
wore make-up poorly, and had little sense of how to wear her hair and dress
neatly. But we began to understand Sarah better as soon as we met with her
mother. Sarah was a living example of her mother's own problems with personal hygiene. Over time, we were able to help Sarah and her mom make a
few changes that at least made her less unpleasant to be around.

I did not see Sarah again until the second quarter of her sophomore year.
She was depressed. Her moods would change like the sun going in and out
of the clouds on a windy day. Mostly, though, it was cloudy.

---

[1] The word *personality* is not used in this book in its technical, psychological sense; here it is a
synonym for character and refers to patterns of relating to others, to attitudes and behaviors
that you can control rather than genetically determined dispositions.

We met together each week for several months, and Sarah began to see her identity and future in a new light. She began to see that God had endowed her with talents that He intended to use in the lives of others. She did not know what they were in any detail, but she began to believe the promises in God's Word—that she could be a productive steward for God if she invested her talents wisely. Through learning this, Sarah became more and more hopeful about her life.

When Sarah and I began to talk, she got C's and D's. As her attitudes changed and stabilized, Sarah slowly improved to the point where she got B's and C's, although she never made it to the honor roll in high school. Her newly dawning identity gave her hope, even if it didn't transform her natural academic ability. When she came to me, she was not popular, attractive, athletic, musical, or artistic. Counseling did not change these features about her, but something did begin to change.

As her confidence grew, Sarah talked to her pastor and became an assistant in a primary Sunday school class. In the summer after her sophomore year, she helped with a Bible school class and led the whole group of children in Bible memory work. At school in her junior year she began to search out others who she thought seemed to have some of the same kinds of needs she used to have. She began to meet with them and to plan parties, Bible studies, and prayer times. During these meetings she offered them the same counsel that had helped her. By the time Sarah graduated, she had befriended and discipled more than a dozen other girls and guys. She was no more "cool" when she took her diploma as a senior than she had been as a smelly freshman, but she was far more stable, influential, and happy.

Sarah's personality qualities, refined and empowered by the Holy Spirit, sent positive shock waves into many of her needy peers at school and young children in her church. She organized, inspired, befriended, cared for, led, planned, taught, and counseled—she became a valuable steward.

All these actions were manifestations of talents that Sarah might have overlooked as she assessed herself for her future career plans. They were not spectacular, standout abilities that many trendy members of the in crowd would value. Yet, as Sarah came to see herself as God saw her and to put herself at His disposal, she experienced a fullness, joy, and confidence in her last high school years. As she came to view herself in this new way and began to involve herself actively in her friends' lives, Sarah gained some fuel for wise decision making about her future.

Character Is God's Priority

In his list of pastoral requirements in 1 Timothy 3:1–13 and Titus 1:5–9, Paul teaches that one's character is critical for church leadership. Out of more than 20 qualities he mentions, only two are skill related: the leader must be able to teach and to manage. The rest of the qualifications are character traits such as self-discipline, gentleness, orderliness, kindness, and discernment. And, although these qualities are expected of church leaders specifically, they are qualities that all of us should emulate. As effective stewards for the Lord, whatever our occupation may be, our success depends not so much on our skills as on our character.

Solomon had many outstanding skills, experiences, and privileges, but his wise and prudent character was what made him most valuable to countless generations. Lydia's business sense (Acts 16:14) may have helped her meet her family's financial needs, but it was her teachability and hospitality that persuaded Paul to spend extra time in ministry among her family and friends. Dorcas worked with textiles, but it was not her designer styles that were most valued by the believers in Joppa (Acts 9:36–39). It was her ability to see people's needs and to reach out to them.

You need to focus on your own personality—what character qualities do you have? Those qualities are as much a part of your talents as anything else, and in fact they are the most important part. Aspects of your personality will give you opportunities to serve and edify others in a unique way. And ironically when you find your skills inadequate, you will also find, like Paul, a special strength: "My power is made perfect in weakness." (2 Corinthians 12:9)

Psychologists have identified as many as 18,000 different personality traits. Obviously, you do not need to think in such detail, but by reflecting on your personality, you may see how certain character traits affect your ability to serve. (And it's important to remember that knowing your weaknesses can be as important for good stewardship as knowing your strengths.) As you come to know yourself better, you may find certain opportunities for service that you have taken for granted. Such self-scrutiny will enable you to cultivate these newly discovered opportunities and to serve God better.

Exploring Your Personality Qualities

1. Check each of the following character qualities for which you have been complimented or noticed, or that you think have made you helpful in others' lives.

_____adaptable	_____aggressive	_____ambitious
_____animated	_____attractive	_____calm
_____carefree	_____caring	_____cheerful
_____clever	_____competitive	_____confident
_____conscientious	_____controlled	_____creative
_____decisive	_____dependable	_____dignified
_____determined	_____disciplined	_____diplomatic
_____discreet	_____efficient	_____energetic
_____enterprising	_____enthusiastic	_____expressive
_____extroverted	_____flexible	_____youthful
_____friendly	_____gentle	_____giving
_____gregarious	_____hardworking	_____honest
_____humorous	_____imaginative	_____independent
_____innovative	_____inspiring	_____intellectual
_____introverted	_____kind	_____trustful
_____lively	_____logical	_____loyal
_____mature	_____methodical	_____meticulous
_____cooperative	_____observant	_____optimistic
_____organized	_____systematic	_____patient
_____perceptive	_____personable	_____persuasive
_____pleasant	_____practical	_____precise
_____punctual	_____questioning	_____quiet
_____rational	_____realistic	_____relaxed
_____reliable	_____respectful	_____responsible
_____secure	_____self-motivated	_____sensitive
_____serious	_____sincere	_____sociable
_____stable	_____supportive	_____organizer
_____tactful	_____tolerant	_____leader
_____tough	_____wise	_____follower

2. Look over the qualities you have checked and group them with others that look somewhat similar. For example, you may wish to group *sensitive* and *supportive* together if you checked both as qualities that others have recognized in you. Some of the qualities may be in more than one group; others may be by themselves.

Group 1

_____

_____

_____

_____

Group 2

_____

_____

_____

_____

Group 3

_____

_____

_____

_____

Group 4

_____

_____

_____

_____

Group 5

_____

_____

_____

_____

Group 6

_____

_____

_____

_____

Group 7

_____

_____

_____

_____

Group 8

_____

_____

_____

_____

Group 9

_____

_____

_____

_____

3. Select three to five of the above groups and give a Summary Trait Title to each group. Your title may be one of the words in the group or a different word that combines the meaning of all three. Write your title in the spaces that follow:

    Example: Jeff was able to group his most evident traits into these groups and assign them the following titles:

Group of Traits	Summary Trait Title
adaptable	
flexible	adaptable
tolerant	
friendly	
extroverted	
pleasant	personable
personable	
sociable	
hardworking	hardworking

Now, you group and summarize your selected traits. (Note: there is not a right or wrong way to do this. You can change your mind about a trait or trait title at any time.)

Group of Traits	Summary Trait Title
Group A	

Group B

_____

_____

_____   _____

_____

_____

Group C

_____

_____

_____   _____

_____

_____

Group D

_____

_____

_____   _____

_____

_____

Group E

_____

_____

_____   _____

_____

_____

_____

4. Write your Summary Trait Titles in the *Personality* section of your personal Career Stewardship Profile on page 174. After Jeff completed the *Personality* section, his CSP looked this:

Jeff's Career Stewardship Profile

Note: This diagram will make more sense as you progress through the Interacts in the rest of the talent clue chapters (9–14).

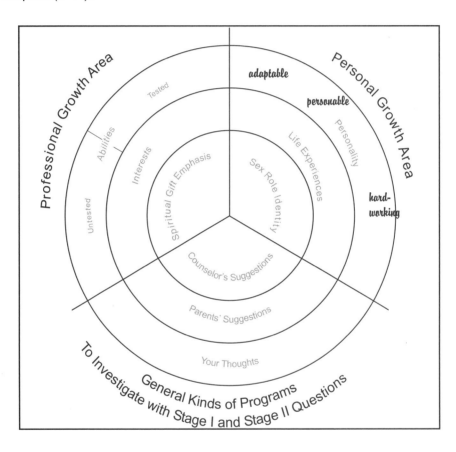

chapter nine

Clues to Your Talents: Your Experiences

What are some important experiences you have had, and how have they helped make you the person you are today?

Your Experiences Are Unique

God has designed a unique set of experiences to help shape every Christian's life. You may be from a single-parent home, or you may have some very difficult family problems. You may have a minority, ethnic, or racial heritage. You may have a learning disability or a physical handicap. Most of us are tempted to view our tough circumstances as misfortunes, but God's plan is to use them all to equip us to fulfill His purposes. God provides all His servants with specific life experiences, good and bad, that form a significant part of their total talent portfolio.

Edward grew up for fifteen of his eighteen years in Haiti, the son of American missionaries. He has been in foreign schools nearly all his life; and although he has American citizenship, he does not feel at home here. When his folks come to the states for furlough, people welcome him "home." But home for Edward is really Haiti, where his friends, church, and school are the sights and sounds, customs, and lifestyle with which he is comfortable.

Now Edward is thinking about his future. Graduation is eight months away, and he is turning his thoughts toward his career plans. He has no idea what to do. He is a typical student in most respects, though his math and science performance have been less than average, and his knowledge of American social issues is weak.

In a seminar for missionary kids, Edward had a chance to express his confusion: "I feel as if I really don't fit anywhere. I don't have any idea how to plan because I don't think I can do anything. I don't even have a strong feeling about what I would like to do."

"Is it an accident that you have grown up in the Haitian culture, Ed?" I asked.

"No, I guess not. I know that God is supposed to be in control of everything, but how does that help me make any definite plans for next year or for life?"

Ed needed to give some thought to the unique experiences God had given him in Haiti. Ephesians 2:10 says that Christians are "God's workmanship, created in Christ Jesus to do good works, which God prepared in advance for us to do." God was fashioning Ed for work that He had planned for him to do from eternity. Like all of us, Ed needed to look at his circumstances and ask himself what God had been equipping him for with his special set of experiences.

Ed's experiences were just another part of those talents that God had blessed him with. As a result of his experiences, Ed could speak French and Creole. His experiences of living in a different culture, and watching his dad minister there, made him sensitive to the needs of people in other cultures. The terrible poverty in Haiti helped him see what real need is.

Still, Ed wasn't sure how these experiences could translate into career plans. With time, however, he came to recognize that God doesn't expect His children to know what they are going to do for the rest of their lives. After a couple of years at a Christian college with an undeclared major, Ed decided that the wisest way for him to use his background was through foreign service in the diplomatic corps. He thought he might consider missions work later on.

It is likely that Ed's experiences were totally unlike yours. Most of us don't grow up with experience in a foreign culture that we need to relate to our career plans. But all of us have experiences that are important for faithful and wise career stewardship.

Your Experiences Are Not Accidental

A few years ago, I met a young married couple who said they were professional picture framers. They both had master's degrees in art and spent their summers in Europe and Britain visiting and studying in art galleries and museums. I was perplexed. Wasn't all this advanced training a kind of overkill, considering their business was just picture framing? When I asked them about it, they just laughed and said that I really did not understand what their business involved. They explained that when someone takes a picture to them, they study the work and research the artist. They try to determine the message of the work and then design, select materials, and build the frame they believe will most clearly help to communicate the artist's purpose.

This is what God does with his people. "We are God's workmanship, created in Christ Jesus to do good works...." (Ephesians 2:10) We are His project—His picture—and the experiences He allows to come into our lives are His artistically planned frame. Paul tells us that God sovereignly determines even the boundaries of our living situations: "From one man He made every nation of men, that they should inhabit the whole earth;

and He determined the times set for them and the exact places where they should live." (Acts 17:26)

We like to quote Romans 8:28 to bring comfort to believers who are facing serious difficulties: "And we know that in all things God works for the good of those who love him." And this verse comforts us because it speaks of God's controlling love in our lives. Somehow, according to His wise, loving, and powerful purposes, God involves Himself with every experience we have. Yet He creates us with wills that set us apart from animals and robots.

Our experiences are not accidents or simply hurdles to overcome so that we can get on with the next part of our lives. They are some of the building blocks, the raw materials, out of which He wants to construct a sound career stewardship plan.

Will's high school experience with Young Life (a Christian youth ministry and outreach in public high schools) whetted his appetite for working with young people. He got involved in many kids' lives and saw firsthand the brokenness and heartache that some live with. Today, he is a social worker specializing in drug- and alcohol-related problems.

Rose had an abortion while she was in high school. After several years, after committing herself to Christ, and a husband and two children later, Rose pursued special training in counseling. Now she is doing effective post-abortion and evangelism counseling in a Christian crisis pregnancy center.

Wendy comes from a family of eighteen kids. She has had five biological brothers and sisters, and twelve other adopted and long-term foster care brothers and sisters. Her pursuit of a pediatric nursing career emerges from her rich well of experience in a large family.

Sometimes, experiences seem to provide a young person with clear occupational alternatives. Often, though, they work together with other clues to point toward a path of faithful career stewardship. You must not ignore the experiences that God has given you. They are not accidental. If you are a believer, they are very much a part of the "all things" that Paul says "God works for the good of those who love Him." (Romans 8:28) They are part of that complete set of resources God has entrusted to us, a portion of those talents that we must completely invest.

God has given you a unique spectrum of experiences. You may have considered some, like your sex, race, home background, and economic or cultural disadvantages or opportunities to be a major handicap. But God's involvement in your life guarantees that there are no accidents in your background. Your experiences affect your talents. They are God's framework within which He intends you to function as His "workmanship." (Ephesians 2:10)

The exercises here will help you uncover talents that your experiences may show you to have.

Step One

Write a description of at least one paragraph about your memorable experiences in each area described. While it will take some time to do this exercise well, the more thoroughly you write about your experiences, the more helpful this will be for you. Many have written several pages in each area—not simply a paragraph—and have gained helpful insights about themselves for their career planning.

Jeff's example of Summary 1:

All through my childhood my family moved from place to place. I was in seven different schools before I was in ninth grade. Our family learned to pull together through these unsettled times of packing and unpacking—especially when Mom was expecting one of my brothers or sisters. I remember one time when my dad came home looking very sad. We had been living on that base for only four months. I told him that, if we had to move again, I was sure the Lord would be with us. He brightened up immediately and seemed to be a different person.

Now you follow Jeff's example. Summarize several experiences in each of the following areas. Use as much space as necessary.

1. Summary of early-life experiences (before high school):

_____

_____

_____

_____

_____

_____

_____

_____

_____

_____

2. Summary of high school experiences:

    a. extracurricular experiences

_____

_____

_____

_____

    b. social experiences

_____

_____

_____

_____

    c. classroom experiences

_____

_____

_____

_____

    d. other experiences

_____

_____

_____

_____

3. Summary of travel experiences:

_____

_____

_____

_____

_____

_____

_____

_____

_____

_____

_____

4. Summary of church-related social experiences:

_____

_____

_____

_____

_____

_____

_____

_____

_____

_____

_____

5. Summary of Christian service and ministry experiences:

_____

_____

_____

_____

_____

_____

_____

_____

_____

6. Summary of music/athletic/outdoor experiences:

_____

_____

_____

_____

_____

_____

_____

_____

_____

7. Summary of leisure-time/hobby experiences:

_____

_____

_____

_____

_____

_____

8. Summary of honor and recognition experiences:

_____

_____

_____

_____

_____

_____

_____

_____

_____

9. Summary of experiences with projects and special tasks:

_____

_____

_____

_____

_____

_____

_____

_____

_____

_____

10. Summary of work experiences:

_____

_____

_____

_____

_____

_____

_____

_____

_____

_____

11. Summary of other experiences that come to your mind:

_____

_____

_____

_____

_____

_____

_____

_____

_____

_____

Step Two

Go back and reread each paragraph you wrote. Think through the experiences you described, and identify any abilities or skills you may have shown.

In the margin next to each paragraph, write one to three words summarizing talents that your experiences may point to. The following list suggests some talents to look for. You may sometimes repeat a word, since you probably showed the same skills and abilities in more than one experience.

Sample abilities, interests, personality qualities (talents)

• accounting	• acting	• adapting
• analyzing	• assembling	• building
• competing	• classifying	• calculating
• compiling	• composing	• cooperating
• coordinating	• counseling	• creating
• dealing	• making decisions	• designing
• developing ideas	• developing projects	• directing
• editing	• showing empathy	• encouraging
• evaluating	• evaluating people	• examining projects
• being flexible	• showing foresight	• informing
• following directions	• initiating	• innovating
• inspiring	• instructing	• leading
• lecturing	• managing	• manipulating
• marketing	• motivating	• negotiating
• organizing	• planning	• predicting
• persuading	• solving problems	• programming
• promoting	• having rapport	• relating
• researching	• resolving conflicts	• being sensitive
• serving	• systematizing	• supervising
• teaching	• trusting	• writing

© *2001*

Step Three

Summarize your findings.

a. Look closely at the words you wrote in the margin next to each paragraph. Circle the word in each group that best summarizes the talents you listed. Then write your circled words below.

_____   _____   _____

_____   _____   _____

b. Copy your key summary words from *a* in the "Life Experiences" section of your CSProfile on page 174.

    After Jeff had filled in the "Life Experiences" section of his CSProfile, it looked like the example below. Your own CSProfile may include more words or fewer words than Jeff's.

Jeff's Career Stewardship Profile

chapter ten

Clues to Your Talents: Your Career Planning as a Young Woman

A flood of bewildering advice from our culture swirls around modern young women, often confusing them about what it means to be a woman. "Who am I?" Sue asked. "Everyone tells me I should think about college and an occupation, but what I really want is a husband and a family to care for. I get the feeling that if I think about marriage and children, I am somehow committing myself to a dungeon. What am I supposed to do?"

Some of the problems in our world—sexual exploitation of women, single-parent families, men who abdicate their responsibilities to a wife and children, marital troubles and divorce, open homosexuality, two-career households, workaholism, and treating sex roles as matters of arbitrary choice—combine to confuse young men and women about who they are, how they ought to relate to each other, and what they ought to expect from each other.

Amid this swirling sea, the Bible offers some sure ground. In this chapter and the next, we will see that God has designed sexual differences for a purpose, and that He has not left us in the dark about how our sexual identity should affect our life planning. Your identity as a woman is no accident—you are God's creation in every way: "For You created my inmost being; You knit me together in my mother's womb." (Psalm 139:13) After reading this chapter, you should be closer to understanding how a faithful steward should think about himself or herself in today's confused and confusing culture.

Eve's Example

God created Eve as Adam's "suitable helper." (Genesis 2:18) She received the title "woman" because "she was taken out of man" (Genesis 2:23), and she was named Eve "because she would become the mother of all the living." (Genesis 3:20) Much of Eve's identity came from her relation to others: she was Adam's helper, and she was named for her role of mothering all mankind. The Lord describes Eve as a "suitable helper," emphasizing her position as a counterpart. Eve is God's example to all women. She provides a pattern of behavior, a sex role, that is followed by godly women throughout Scripture. Through her example, God stresses two important aspects of a woman's identity: her nature as a complement or helper (as seen in her marital relation to her husband) and her nature as a nurturer (as seen in her motherly relation to her children).

By way of Eve's example, then, God's Word teaches that it would be wise for women to make their career plans with their future roles as wives and mothers clearly in mind. God does not require women to marry and bear children, nor does he require women to select a career that will include marriage and motherhood. In other words, not every woman should, or must, marry and raise a family. But He does teach that, in general, a woman's very nature encourages her to marry and be a mother, and that these roles are important in her life. As a result, wise young women will consider their probable future roles as wife and mother when they make their career plans.

Similar Abilities

While women are given distinct roles as wives and mothers, God's Word will not allow us to view either sex as inferior to the other. On the contrary, Scripture shows that women and men are equally capable of doing nearly everything. According to Scripture, women, as well as men, can do the following:

- work outside the home (the woman of Proverbs 31; Lydia in Acts 16:14)
- govern, strategize, and fight (Deborah in Judges 4)
- manage (Esther in the book of Esther; young widows in 1 Timothy 5:14)
- provide sole support for a household (Ruth in the book of Ruth; Hagar in Genesis 21)
- run their own business while balancing it effectively with running a household (Lydia in Acts 16:15; the woman in Proverbs 31)
- help others materially (Dorcas in Acts 9:36; the woman in Proverbs 31)
- instruct (Priscilla in Acts 18:26; older women in Titus 2; the woman of Proverbs 31:26)
- pray (women of Jerusalem in Acts 1:14; women of Corinth in 1 Corinthians 11:5)
- advise (Abigail in 1 Samuel 25; Esther in Esther 5, 8)
- serve the church (Phoebe in Romans 16; widows in 1 Timothy 5:9,10)

Some people assume that men can do these things, but doubt that women can do them as effectively. God's Word directly contradicts such assumptions by providing many examples of women with diverse abilities. Such similarities do not mean that the roles of men and women are identical, nor do they mean that men and women will want to do, or ought to do, all the same things. However, they do show that men and women are able to perform many similar kinds of work. Sexual identity does not limit women from performing a wide variety of tasks effectively.

Tragically, men have traditionally demeaned or exploited women for their complementary and nurturing roles. In doing so, men rebel against God. They show contempt for God's command to recognize a woman's dignity and to show her respect. Because of the frequency of such abuses, the church has come under heavy, and often deserved, criticism from feminists. Unfortunately, feminists rarely sort out the abuses from the principles, and as a result they commonly condemn Christianity as a religion of oppression.

Such criticisms often intimidate and confuse young women who, like Sue in the opening paragraph of this chapter, want to be faithful to Christ but do not want to "sell out" their womanhood. Women must not be intimidated by a movement that ignores or denies the dignity of the differences God has created. Instead, they should have confidence in their natural inclinations toward caring and nurturing, knowing that such desires were created in them.

Women on the Job

Historically, men have not only disparaged motherhood; they have also stifled women, allowing them scant responsibility and little freedom outside the home. Today, men and women alike need to recognize the breadth of women's talents. As our next example from Scripture will show, a woman's capacity to nurture does not strip her of other skills or narrow her options.

The virtuous woman of Proverbs 31:10–31 combined being a wife and mother with real estate development (v. 16), marketing (v. 18), and sales (v. 24). Meanwhile, the praise that she received from her husband and children assures us that she had not neglected her family: "Her children arise and call her blessed, her husband also, and he praises her." (v. 28) Having chosen the role of wife and mother, this woman kept her priorities in line with God's and didn't neglect her primary responsibility to care for and love her family.

At the same time, she took full advantage of her talents and pursued a variety of occupational paths with much success. She didn't think of herself as imprisoned in a dungeon called "wife and mother." Instead, she channeled the wide range of her talents into work roles that were compatible with her primary work of helping her husband and nurturing her children. She committed her life to the most significant work anyone can do, preparing people to live as whole, healthy, and spiritually mature servants of the living God.

According to the Bureau of Labor and Statistics, 60 percent of all women in America over 20 years old work outside the home. One woman in Christian work observed that "for seven out of ten of these women, working is necessary. Forty-three percent are the sole support for themselves and their dependents, and another 28 percent are married to men earning less than $10,500 per year."

An article in the *Los Angeles Times* quoted a government estimate that "a girl born in 1980 is likely to spend 29.4 years of her adult life on the job ... compared to 38.9 years for boys." Tragically, high divorce rates, the necessity of earning two incomes to meet the rising costs of living, and the fact that adults are getting married later in life are real forces that make it wise for a young woman to make plans for an occupation.

Striking the Proper Balance: How Should a Young Woman Plan?

The virtuous woman of Proverbs 31 had a family that praised her and honored her. She used her talents in a wide range of ways to serve her family and others. Likewise, today's young women ought to keep their occupational plans adaptable to the possibility of marriage and children.

Unfortunately, Martha has to make some adjustments. She is a 37-year-old mother of two school-age children. She has been trying to keep her stock exchange job in balance with her family responsibilities, but she is struggling. "When I'm at work, I constantly think about my children and husband. I'm bothered by the guilt of the unfinished work at home and the fact that I am not in any condition to give them my full attention when I get home. When I'm at home, I struggle to be altogether there. My mind drifts to the unfinished work at the exchange."

If you marry, will you be able to meet the demands of your chosen profession, on the one hand, and the demands of marriage and a family, on the other? Will you be able to subordinate your occupation to your role as a wife and mother, following the Proverbs 31 pattern? Living with this kind of balance is usually possible, but sadly it is rare. Young women and their parents often give little forethought to their God-designed identity and work-role options. To be a faithful steward, you need to give careful thought to your career plans and your sex role. The whole-life prosperity that God grants to young women who are faithful stewards is certain and always without regret or guilt.

Young women need to be honest with themselves and aware of their desires and their culture's pressures. A faithful steward will ask herself, "If I pursue this occupational direction and choose to marry and have a family, can I subordinate my professional work to my role as a wife and mother? Or would this field demand that I subordinate my family role to my profession?" Because of our sinful nature, the most natural tendency will be to turn God's order upside down. A faithful steward will insist that she put her family above her work, not her work above her family. God's design for the family, and for a woman's role in it, makes the first alternative necessary and the second foolish: "The wise woman builds her house; but with her hands, the foolish one tears hers down." (Proverbs 14:1)

Martha found that balance very difficult to achieve. Another woman with a different personality might not have the conflict she had and might be able to strike a better balance between family and career.

Tina is a young woman trying to be realistic about the occupational pressures she will probably face. In high school, she has been on the honor roll, and her performance in her advanced placement courses has revealed her above-average academic ability. She has an interest in helping people and has had an interest in medicine for as long as she can remember. Medicine seems a sensible field for her to explore. But she also has serious plans for marriage and a family, so she's asking whether these can fit in with her professional hopes. Should her womanhood be a serious factor in her plans? How should her dreams for marriage and a family, or even her nature as a woman, affect her career aspirations? In her desire to be a faithful steward, she has begun well by being willing to ask herself these questions.

Thinking this way can be difficult in a culture such as ours that denigrates women who choose to accept a family role patterned after God's priorities. Women who plan with these values in mind are often the objects of misguided pity and even scorn in college and university settings. When she was to be the commencement speaker at an exclusive women's college, former First Lady Barbara Bush was scorned by many of the university women because she willingly accepted her identity as a wife and mother. In response, she was not intimidated but insisted that such a role had dignity and significance of its own.

As a faithful and wise steward, you must commit yourself to make career plans like the woman of Proverbs 31, who feared the Lord (v. 30). The other form of fear, "the fear of man," is a "snare" or trap. (Proverbs 29:25) The intimidating sneers and promises of our modern culture will urge you to bury, away from consciousness, the talents that emerge from your womanhood. But, as you pursue the path that God calls you to, you can expect to experience fulfillment and prosperity.

No passage of Scripture is more descriptive of the balanced life of a fulfilled and fulfilling woman than Proverbs 31. This exercise is intended to help you think about how this virtuous woman balanced her life. The Proverbs 31 woman also provides a model for you to imitate as you proceed with your career stewardship planning.

Step One

Read each verse and circle the letter or letters under each that identify the role(s) in which the virtuous woman seems to be serving.

Key: P—her personal life, M—her marital role, F—her family role, W—her work (or occupational) role, S—her social role

Proverbs 31:10–31

P M F W S (v10) "A wife of noble character who can find? She is worth far more than rubies."

P M F W S (v11) "Her husband has full confidence in her and lacks nothing of value."

P M F W S (v12) "She brings him good, not harm, all the days of her life."

P M F W S (v13) "She selects wool and flax and works with eager hands."

P M F W S (v14) "She is like the merchant ships, bringing her food from afar."

P M F W S (v15) "She gets up while it is still dark; she provides food for her family and portions for her servant girls."

P M F W S (v16) "She considers a field and buys it; out of her earnings she plants a vineyard."

P M F W S (v17) "She sets about her work vigorously; her arms are strong for her tasks."

P M F W S (v18) "She sees that her trading is profitable, and her lamp does not go out at night."

P M F W S (v19) "In her hand she holds the distaff and grasps the spindle with her fingers."

P M F W S (v20) "She opens her arms to the poor and extends her hands to the needy."

P M F W S (v21) "When it snows, she has no fear for her household; for all of them are clothed in scarlet."

P M F W S (v22) "She makes coverings for her bed; she is clothed in fine linen and purple."

P M F W S (v23) "Her husband is respected at the city gate, where he takes his seat among the elders of the land."

P M F W S (v24) "She makes linen garments and sells them, and supplies the merchants with sashes."

P M F W S (v25) "She is clothed with strength and dignity; she can laugh at the days to come."

P M F W S (v26) "She speaks with wisdom, and faithful instruction is on her tongue."

P M F W S (v27) "She watches over the affairs of her household and does not eat the bread of idleness."

P M F W S (v28) "Her children arise and call her blessed; her husband also, and he praises her."

P M F W S (v29) "Many women do noble things, but you surpass them all."

P M F W S (v30) "Charm is deceptive, and beauty is fleeting; but a woman who fears the Lord is to be praised."

P M F W S (v31) "Give her the reward she has earned, and let her works bring her praise at the city gate."

Step Two

Now list the verse numbers relating to each different role on the line beside the role names below (the same verse number may be listed beside more than one role).

P _____

M _____

F _____

W _____

S _____

Step Three

What did this woman's priorities seem to be? By the amount of attention (number of verses suggesting each role), the writer gives priority to each of these areas. What does the order of her priorities appear to be?

First Priority: _____

Second Priority: _____

Third Priority: _____

Fourth Priority: _____

Fifth Priority: _____

Step Four

"Being a wife and mother is going to be such a bore! What a waste of my talents!"

Would the wife and mother of Proverbs 31 have said this? Why or why not?

Read Proverbs 31:10–31 again. Scan all the descriptive terms below, and place a check mark or the verse number in the space beside each item that describes something she might be doing.

_____Paying bills	_____Building things	_____Competing
_____Coordinating	_____Counseling	_____Creating
_____Dealing	_____Making decisions	_____Designing
_____Developing ideas	_____Developing projects	_____Showing empathy
_____Evaluating people	_____Examining	_____Sewing
_____Planning ahead	_____Initiating	_____Informing
_____Innovating	_____Instructing	_____Inspiring
_____Leading	_____Cooking	_____Managing
_____Negotiating	_____Organizing	_____Planning
_____Gossiping	_____Solving problems	_____Promoting
_____Feeling rapport	_____Researching	_____Selling
_____Resolving conflicts	_____Serving others	_____Speaking
_____Supervising	_____Teaching	_____Persuading

Step Five

If you were the counselor for the young woman mentioned at the beginning of step four, what suggestions would you give her for her career planning after graduation? How would you encourage her to think about occupational planning if she said that she hoped marriage and family matters would be in her future?

_____

_____

_____

_____

_____

_____

Step Six: Your Application

In each of the roles the Proverbs 31 woman sought to fulfill, list one character quality that you would like to develop in your career stewardship as a young woman.

Personal character quality   _____

Marital character quality   _____

Family character quality   _____

Worker/occupational character quality   _____

Social character quality   _____

Record each quality in which you'd like to mature in the "Sex Role Identity" section of your CSProfile on page 174.

chapter eleven

Clues to Your Talents: Your Career Planning as a Young Man

What does it mean to be a man? What is manliness? How should your identity as a young man affect your career planning?

Seeing Through the Fog

Our culture broadcasts its images of a young man through every known medium. It confuses and frustrates boys with many of its Hollywood stereotypes of manliness ranging from the cool cop, to the tough champion, to the sensual man of the world. Any of these stereotypes, combined with the common cynical attitudes that depict sensitivity to spiritual matters as an effeminate weakness, help create an identity fog that is difficult for many young men to see through.

This fog hinders them from developing a clear view of how they should make their career plans. It is especially thick when young men lack positive male role models in their own families, as is the case for nearly half today (in single-parent families, for example). This fog often undermines a young man's motivation to grow spiritually by keeping his important identity as a leader in the background. When we have a distorted idea about what it means to be a man, and when we play down, ignore, or deny our God-created sex differences, we overlook an important part of the total constellation of our talents.

Historic biblical Christianity has recognized that young men have a special accountability for exercising spiritual leadership in the home and in the church. How many youth groups, church ministries, mission ministries, and Christian homes are led by godly women pleading for men to get involved and show leadership initiative? Thankfully, God has raised up many younger and older women who try to fill the gaps. Many do extraordinary work, but one sex cannot completely satisfy roles that God intended two sexes to fulfill together.

God has designed men to exercise their responsibilities as leaders, providers, and protectors in the family (Ephesians 5:22–33) and in the church. (1 Timothy 3; Titus 1) This does not mean women are without leadership capability or responsibility. But God has delegated the final responsibility for godly leadership to men.

The Here and Now

So, what does this have to do with young men who are still in school and who are neither married nor church leaders?

What you will be, you are now becoming. As you are being married, or as your wife delivers your first child, you will not be magically transformed from a spiritually lazy man into a mature and godly one, or from a self-indulgent steward into a faithful and wise one. Neither marriage nor parenthood will change your basic character.

Your present maturity as a Christian young man will influence how well you fill your future roles. "Godliness," Paul said, "has value for all things, holding promise for both the present life and the life to come." (1 Timothy 4:8) Growth in godliness is important for everyone, but a young man who seeks to be holy will find himself well prepared for his future roles as a husband, father, and church leader. If you are casual now about your personal quiet time, your service in the church, and your giving to the church and to the needy, you are likely to carry these habits into the future. The difference between then and now, however, is that the longer you remain casual about the changes you should make, the more difficult those changes will become. In the future those patterns will be set like concrete. You may still be able to change, but only with difficulty. Often, change requires a painful chipping and breaking that will affect your life and the lives of others you love.

Future Leadership

In 1 Timothy 3:1–7, Paul gives us a list of character qualities that are necessary for leaders in the church. In addition, this list of qualities provides an important look at how God views leadership in general, and what kind of people He wants to use as leaders. Paul is describing the character qualities that spiritually mature young men will seek.

Read the following version of the passage, which comes from the *Amplified New Testament*, and begin to take a spiritual inventory. Are these qualities beginning to show themselves in you?

> *If any man [eagerly] seeks the office of bishop [superintendent, overseer], he desires an excellent task [work]. Now a bishop [superintendent, overseer] must give no grounds for accusation but must be above reproach, the husband of one wife, circumspect and temperate and self-controlled; [he must be] sensible and well-behaved and dignified, and lead an orderly [disciplined] life; [he must be] hospitable—showing love for and being a friend to the believers, especially strangers and foreigners—[and] be a capable and qualified teacher, not given to wine, not combative but gentle and considerate, not quarrelsome but forbearing and peaceable, and not a lover of money—insatiable for wealth and ready to obtain it by questionable means. He must rule his own household well, keeping his children under control, with true dignity, commanding their respect in every way and keeping them respectful. For if a man does not know how to rule his own household, how is he to take care of the church of God? He must not be a new convert, or he may [develop a beclouded and stupid state of mind] as the result of pride, [be blinded by] conceit, and fall into the condemnation that the devil [once] did. Furthermore he must have a good reputation and be well thought of by those outside [the church], lest he become involved in slander and incur reproach and fall into the devil's trap.*

You might consider listing each of these qualities and making one per week the theme of your personal prayer requests. God wants these qualities to be maturing in you, for they hold "promise for both the present life and the life to come." (1 Timothy 4:8) The quality of your future life and your faithfulness as a leader depend on how you are progressing toward these virtues now. What you will be, you are now becoming.

Future Leadership in Your Family

Most young men marry. If you decide to get married, you will be accepting the responsibility for the role of leadership in your family—a role that God has designed. Contrary to a popular stereotype of the Bible's teaching, this does not mean you are "king of your castle" with your wife and family existing merely to satisfy your desires. You will be accountable as head of your home, but biblical leadership or "headship" contrasts sharply with these distorted views.

Ephesians 5:22–33 is the most extensive passage in the New Testament to describe what a husband and family leader should look like:

> *Wives, submit to your husbands as to the Lord. For the husband is the head of the wife as Christ is the head of the church, his body, of which he is the Savior. Now as the church submits to Christ, so also wives should submit to their husbands in everything.*

Husbands, love your wives, just as Christ loved the church and gave himself up for her to make her holy, cleansing her by the washing with water through the word, and to present her to himself as a radiant church, without stain or wrinkle or any other blemish, but holy and blameless. In this same way, husbands ought to love their wives as their own bodies. He who loves his wife loves himself. After all, no one ever hated his own body, but he feeds and cares for it, just as Christ does the church—for we are members of His body. "For this reason a man will leave his father and mother and be united to his wife, and the two will become one flesh." This is a profound mystery—but I am talking about Christ and the church. However, each one of you also must love his wife as he loves himself, and the wife must respect her husband.

The style of leadership (headship) Paul urges men to exercise is loving servanthood. The biggest servant in the home is to be the husband and father. This conflicts strongly with our culture's view of leadership. According to the world, leaders are people of power, people who command and delegate. The more important they are, the more they deserve to be served. God's style of leadership is different. It corresponds to Jesus' service in John 13:1–17 when He washed His disciples' feet.

If, as a young man, you focus on maturing in these areas, they will have an impact on your later adult life. When Peter urged young believers to develop a series of character qualities similar to those Paul wrote about in 1 Timothy and Ephesians, he concluded:

For if you possess these qualities in increasing measure, they will keep you from being ineffective and unproductive in your knowledge of our Lord Jesus Christ. But if anyone does not have them, he is nearsighted and blind. (2 Peter 1:8, 9)

Career Planning as a Young Man

Chip was not interested in marriage and didn't think about family or church leadership while he was in high school. He dated around and even had a couple of steady relationships before his junior year in college, when he met the young woman he eventually married. He was involved in his church and youth group, but not because he was conscious of how this would affect his future.

But from Chip's earliest years, his dad had encouraged him to think of himself from God's perspective. His father tried to model sensitivity and a servant spirit in the family and talked openly with Chip about his own failures and those of other dads in these areas. He also led his family in serving others in their church and neighborhood.

Chip wasn't sure how to plan for his future after high school. The best he could do was apply to schools that would help him build on his academic strengths while he continued to think about how to invest his life wisely. But he allowed one other factor to guide his thinking too: spiritual maturity. "I felt I needed to grow up more, spiritually," Chip said. "I needed to put myself into a situation where I would be able to grow in the areas that would be important for a profession, but I also needed to grow in ways that would help me become the man that the Lord wanted me to become."

Chip decided to go to a local Bible college for a year or two because of the mix of liberal arts and Bible-related courses. He figured he could transfer most courses to another college when he wanted to change schools and that his time there would help him mature as a Christian young man. Today, he has a healthy marriage with a wife and two children, and he is active as a college and career group teacher in his church. He also manages a radio station. Chip planned with his sexual identity in mind. He wanted to mature as a young man of God.

You may or may not have been raised with a thoughtful dad like Chip's. But your maleness does make a difference to God. Your sexual identity is no accident. It took God's intervention to create your life, and your sexual identity was part of His plan from the beginning. Do not allow your culture to stifle your zeal to become the kind of young man that God values most highly. Godly character will keep you from being "ineffective and unproductive" in your stewardship of the wide range of your talents.

What you will be, you are now becoming.

These exercises are designed to help you think through your personal identity as a young man. Who are you and who are you becoming? The kind of person you are as a man will have definite bearing on the quality of your career stewardship.

Step One

Read each of the verses and rank yourself on the scale below it. Are you growing in ways that will enable you to be a faithful and wise steward?

Caution: Some of these passages describe what a husband or church leader should be like. The fact is, all these qualities ought to be evident in everyone. Other passages command these character qualities for all Christians. These passages simply indicate the nature of a mature man and what must be true of a church leader. The important point is that if you are not on the way to developing these qualities now, you may not possess them in any degree of maturity later, either.

1. 1 John 2:14b

    "I write to you, young men, because you are strong and the Word of God lives in you, and you have overcome the evil one."

    a. Your strength of character and commitment show up when friends make decisions to do things that you know are wrong for you.

    ❑ not really evident   ❑ inconsistently evident   ❑ generally evident

    b. You want the standards of the Word of God to be lived out among your friends and in your private life.

    ❑ not really evident   ❑ inconsistently evident   ❑ generally evident

    c. You battle with temptation and find yourself overcoming the tempter—not always, of course, but many times.

    ❑ not really evident   ❑ inconsistently evident   ❑ generally evident

2. Ephesians 5:25

"Husbands, love your wives, just as Christ loved the church and gave himself up for her."

Men are to love as Christ did, sacrificially. Your love for a special girl, or for your family (it's the kind of love you show, not the one to whom you show it that is important here) looks out for their benefit, even at cost to your convenience and desire.

❏ not really evident　　　　❏ inconsistently evident　　　　❏ generally evident

3. Ephesians 5:25–27

"Husbands, love your wives, just as Christ loved the church and gave himself up for her … to make her holy, cleansing her by the washing with water through the Word, and to present her to himself as a radiant church, without stain or wrinkle or any other blemish, but holy and blameless."

a. Like Christ, men are to be nurturing, building others up. You use the Word of God in the lives of people close to you, especially young women you date or go out with.

　　❏ not really evident　　　　❏ inconsistently evident　　　　❏ generally evident

b. Christ's sacrifice was for the benefit of His bride, the church. Your efforts are aimed at helping others, especially a girlfriend, to grow and be a better person for Christ. You pray for, encourage, and challenge her.

　　❏ not really evident　　　　❏ inconsistently evident　　　　❏ generally evident

4. 1 Timothy 2:8

"I want men everywhere to lift up holy hands in prayer, without anger or disputing."

All Christians may pray. But there is a special place of responsibility for men to be leaders in this area among believers. You show initiative in prayer when there is an opportunity to pray publicly. You don't have to be coaxed or pushed to pray.

❏ not really evident　　　　❏ inconsistently evident　　　　❏ generally evident

5.   1 Timothy 3:1–13

This passage lists many qualities of the mature man who leads effectively. Each of these is evident, though not present in perfection, in the mature man of God. Rate your progress in each.

a.   v. 2, "above reproach" (v. 7, "a good reputation")
You are not open to blame for consistent flaws that detract from a clear commitment to Christ as Lord of your life.

❏ not really evident   ❏ inconsistently evident   ❏ generally evident

b.   v. 2, "temperate, self-controlled"
You do not have a pattern of going to extremes. You are well-balanced.

❏ not really evident   ❏ inconsistently evident   ❏ generally evident

c.   v. 2, "respectable" (v. 8, "worthy of respect")
You are well-ordered and disciplined. You are not generally disorganized in your life.

❏ not really evident   ❏ inconsistently evident   ❏ generally evident

d.   v. 2, "hospitable" (literally, "a lover of strangers")
You are kind to all types of people, especially those not in the "in" group.

❏ not really evident   ❏ inconsistently evident   ❏ generally evident

e.   v. 3, "not violent, but gentle, not quarrelsome"
You do not lose your temper easily or look for a fight. You react in gentleness to difficult situations and to argumentative people.

❏ not really evident   ❏ inconsistently evident   ❏ generally evident

f.   v. 3, "not a lover of money"
Not everything must have a dollar sign or bring you some benefit for you to be interested in it. There is a clear servant aspect to your spirit.

❏ not really evident   ❏ inconsistently evident   ❏ generally evident

g. v. 9, "keep hold of the deep truths of the faith"
You have a growing knowledge of God's Word—more than Sunday school stories. You find yourself seeking to answer people's questions with the truths of Scripture.

❑ not really evident   ❑ inconsistently evident   ❑ generally evident

6. Proverbs 4:20, 23

"My son ... above all else, guard your heart, for it is the wellspring of life."
You are careful about what you allow to fill your thinking. You give thought to the kind of music you listen to, the programs and movies you watch, and the things you read.

❑ not really evident   ❑ inconsistently evident   ❑ generally evident

7. Proverbs 5:8; 7:25; 13:20

"[About an immoral, suggestive, or flirtatious young woman] Keep to a path far from her, do not go near the door of her house.... Do not let your heart turn to her ways or stray into her paths...."

"He who walks with the wise grows wise, but a companion of fools suffers harm."

You are careful about the character of the girls you date or with whom you are friendliest. The friends you choose to get closest to have attitudes and make choices that show they are serious about God and His will.

❑ not really evident   ❑ inconsistently evident   ❑ generally evident

Step Two

Go back over your ratings and make a list of those you marked as "inconsistently evident" or "not really evident." Keep this list in your Bible and use it as a reminder to pray about the qualities you want the Lord to help you develop.

Step Three

Record three or four of the qualities you'd most like to cultivate in the "Sex Role Identity" section of your CSProfile on page 174.

chapter twelve

Clues to Your Talents: Your School-Related Abilities

Like most young people, you may think that your grades and test scores are the key indicators of your talents. The last few chapters have shown that many of your talents are rooted more deeply in your character, including your personality, your experiences, and even your gender. While your performance in school is important, you should look at it only in addition to these more basic talents. Too often, young adults are like those who live in poverty, unaware that they are heirs to a fortune. You, too, have more talent resources than your report card or GPA may indicate. However, while we have been emphasizing other kinds of talent, it is important to remember that your academic abilities are also part of your talent portfolio.

Test Scores, Grades, and Academic Talents

Throughout your high school years, you have probably had to take standardized tests. The results usually include a math score and a verbal score, which show how you compare with other students across the country.

Randy performed particularly well in these standardized tests. His high scores on the PSAT made him a semifinalist for a National Merit Scholarship, and his SAT scores were in the 1,400s. Randy's math and verbal aptitudes were in the top two percent, better than 98 percent of all the students in his grade throughout the country. But while he performed so well in tests, his grades were barely average, placing him in the lower half of his senior class.

Randy hoped that colleges would pay closest attention to his test scores and not his grades. But for many colleges, student motivation is important. Randy could be in trouble, since his grades suggested a lack of consistent hard work on his part.

Sandra's experience was just the opposite. Her grades were good, but her standardized test scores were only average. "I freeze up, and my mind just goes blank in those tests," she confessed.

Since researchers tend to conclude that high school grades measure a student's future performance better than standardized tests, Sandra would be wise to think of her academic potential in terms of her grades. She shouldn't ignore her test scores, but grades will probably be better predictors for her.

Ted is in an entirely different category from Sandra and Randy. According to his teachers, Ted has academic problems that spring from his weak educational background. Yet he came into my office and started talking about electrical engineering, which made me suspicious. I got his records and we sat down to review them together.

"I'm not sure," he began, "but I was thinking about Drexel, or maybe a Christian college like Geneva since they have engineering."

"What math do you have now, Ted?"

"I'm in Algebra 2."

"I see by looking at your transcript that this is your second time with Algebra 2. How are you doing so far?"

"I think I'm getting a C this semester."

"What's English look like? Are you in AP [Advanced Placement] or British Literature?" (the usual college preparatory courses).

"I'm in Brit Lit. I think I have a B- average."

"How were your SAT scores?"

"They were low. I've taken the SAT twice. My math score this time was 360, and my verbal score was 400. Do you think that will be a problem?"

"Have you tried to find out what schools like Drexel or Geneva require for admission to their technical programs like engineering? Usually they look for high grades and combined math and verbal scores of over 1,100, or at least a math score in the upper 500s or 600s. Your scores are well below the math and verbal 500 averages."

Ted was suffering from one of the symptoms of talentwarp that we encountered in chapter 6: career-planning fantasy. He needed to take a hard, honest look at his grades and his test scores, and get a realistic view of his academic abilities before talking about majors and schools. Ted may not have to give up all thought of a career in a field related to engineering, but he needs to bring his immediate educational goals into line with his past and present academic performance.

Related Abilities: What Tests Don't Measure

If Ted takes a hard look at himself, there is always the danger he could come crashing down to earth, realize that he doesn't have the academic strengths he imagined, and succumb to the other extreme of talentwarp: career-planning despair. Again, the problem would be a typical but misplaced emphasis on academic performance.

In reality, many other abilities are closely related to academics, but they are not as easy to measure by tests and grades. If you don't make much of a showing in your grades and tests, you need to expand your horizons to include these other abilities (as well as the talents mentioned in previous chapters). The following is a list of some abilities that may not be measured very well by tests:

Verbal abilities:

- To write coherently
- To persuade
- To negotiate to an agreement
- To converse and relate with other people easily
- To know two or more languages

Numerical abilities:

- To compute quickly and accurately
- To understand quantitative relationships
- To solve quantitative problems

Social abilities:

- To deal with different types of people
- To relate easily in social situations
- To dress and groom well
- To deal with criticism

Investigative abilities:

- To have an inquiring mind
- To gather information systematically
- To recognize relationships among data

Manual/physical abilities
- To understand the way machines work
- To visualize spatial relationships
- To exercise dexterity and/or strength
- To resist physical fatigue

Creative abilities:
- To create new forms with physical objects
- To tell or write stories
- To sense aesthetic values
- To imagine new relationships in ideas, objects, etc.

Instructional abilities:
- To help others learn or understand
- To clarify or simplify abstract ideas or relationships
- To counsel and to provide other similar helping services

Managerial Abilities:
- To direct others in work
- To organize and plan systematically
- To coordinate resources
- To recognize options and make decisions
- To handle details
- To pursue a task until completion

These are some of the many areas in which you need to assess your strengths and weaknesses. You can probably identify with some of these abilities right away. You may have had people seek your help, compliment you, or encourage you in some of these areas. Take their thoughts into consideration, and you will get a good sense of some academic and nonacademic skills you might have ignored. The Bible urges you to seek this sort of advice from trusted and respected relatives and friends: "Plans fail for lack of counsel, but with many advisers they succeed;" (Proverbs 15:22) and "Make plans by seeking advice; if you wage war, obtain guidance". (Proverbs 20:18)

The plans you make now can have an impact on the rest of your life, and there are many who stand ready to give advice, good and bad, on where to turn. Get advice and counsel from some respected adults (parent, teacher, youth director, pastor, neighbor) to help you be realistic, balanced, and more fully aware of the capabilities God has entrusted to you. If you limit your abilities to those measured by grades and tests, you may be pursuing too narrow a career plan for the steward God has made you to be.

School-related abilities will affect your success in the next level of education you choose. These alone won't determine your occupational success. However, schools and colleges will use what they know of your school-related abilities to decide whether or not to admit you to their program for training.

You have taken many tests of your school-related abilities up to this point in your life. Some have been designed to tell you how strong your abilities are in different areas—especially verbal and mathematical. These are the more easily measured talents. But not all abilities are as easy to test and measure as these two. The following exercises concern two types of school-related ablities, easily measured (tested) and not easily measured (usually untested).

How to Determine Your School-Related Abilities

1. Abilities That Tests Measure

    Review your standardized test scores with a counselor or adviser in your school. (Standardized tests are those in which students use special test booklets and answer sheets, and teachers read specially prepared instructions. Often these tests are timed.)

    a. Look for a pattern of strengths or weaknesses in your scores. Ask your counselor to help you spot them.

    b. With your counselor or adviser, try to determine whether your pattern of strengths or weaknesses is the result of abilities or other factors. For example, some kids were sick a lot in the year the tests were given. Some were going through some hard home problems. Some may have simply been immature and have goofed off a lot.

    c. With these trends in mind, ask your counselor to help you determine what kind of school or program is realistic for you to think about attending after high school. (Kinds of programs may include four-year colleges, community colleges, trade or technical schools, institutes, secretarial schools, hospital technology programs.) Note: Your counselor may want to press you to decide "what you are interested in" before talking about schools. Your goal here is not specific schools, but the kind of schools in which your tested abilities indicate you can probably succeed. So your occupational interests are not necessary at this point.

d. Write your conclusion about your pattern of tested abilities in the "Abilities Tested" in the "Professional Growth Area" segment of your CSProfile.

e. Write your counselor's or adviser's kind-of-school recommendations in the "Counselor's Suggestions" segment of "General Kinds of Programs" in your CSProfile on page 174.

2. Abilities That Tests Don't Measure Well

Scan each of the eight ability areas below. Mark all the skills in which you believe you (or a class-mate you are encouraging) have had some success. List two or three experiences for each skill you check that seem to support your opinion.

1. Verbal abilities:
   - To write coherently
   - To persuade
   - To negotiate to an agreement
   - To converse and relate with other people easily
   - To know two or more languages

2. Numerical abilities:
   - To compute quickly and accurately
   - To understand quantitative relationships
   - To solve quantitative problems

3. Social abilities:
   - To deal with different types of people
   - To relate easily in social situations
   - To dress and groom well
   - To deal with criticism

4. Investigative abilities:
   - To have an inquiring mind
   - To gather information systematically
   - To recognize relationships among data

5. Manual/physical abilities
   - To understand the way machines work
   - To visualize spatial relationships
   - To show dexterity and/or strength
   - To resist physical fatigue

6. Creative abilities:
   - To create new forms with physical objects
   - To tell or write stories
   - To sense aesthetic values
   - To imagine new relationships in ideas, objects, etc.

7. Instructional abilities:
   - To help others learn or understand
   - To clarify or simplify abstract ideas or relationships
   - To counsel, and to provide other similar helping services

8. Managerial abilities:
   - To direct others in work
   - To organize and plan systematically
   - To coordinate resources
   - To recognize and make decisions
   - To handle details
   - To pursue a task until completion

3. Advice and Counsel

Talk to your parents and at least one other respected adult (such as a youth pastor or teacher). You don't have to agree with their conclusions. But God has put them in your life, and their experience with you should give them some sense of your strengths and weaknesses.

   a. Ask them to look over this list (on the previous pages) and identify the skills in the ability areas that they think you have. Have them write down their reasons for their opinions. Don't let them see your own list yet. Ask for their help without telling them how you see things.

   b. With these skills in mind, ask your parents and the other respected adult to help you determine what kind of school or program is realistic for you to think about attending after high school. (Kinds of programs may include four-year colleges, community colleges, trade or technical schools, institutes, secretarial schools, hospital technology programs.) Note: Keep in mind the caution above. You don't need to know what you are interested in for this exercise. It's the general kind of school you are seeking their counsel about at this time.

c. List the ability areas in which you, your parents, and your other adult friend(s) agree that you have strengths. Write them in the section marked "Abilities, Untested" in the "Professional Growth Area" segment of your CSProfile on page 174.

d. Write your parents' and other respected adults' kind-of-school recommendations in the "General Kinds of Programs" segment of your CSProfile.

chapter thirteen

Clues to Your Talents: Your Interests

In chapter 2, we told you about a school counselor who said he found an easy, biblical way to help young people determine God's will for their lives: "I just ask them what they want to do," he said, "and God's will for them is always the opposite." He was right about only one thing: it was easy; but his method was far from biblical. Interests have their limitations, but they are also an important part of your personality and do not need to be looked on with suspicion or completely dismissed, as this counselor did. He assumed that if a young person was interested in going into medicine, for example, it was because of the prestige and wealth of the profession. Such cynicism and stereotyping have little place in God's approach to career planning.

Having Interests and Following Christ

Most counselors tend to go to the opposite extreme and give interests too much priority. This counselor stripped them of all usefulness. His negativism is fed by many professing Christians who pursue occupational goals and make educational plans but do not seem to take seriously the value Jesus gives to self-denial when He says, "If anyone would come after me, he must deny himself and take up his cross daily and follow me." (Luke 9:23) Again, Jesus says,

> *"If anyone comes to me and does not hate his father and mother, his wife and children, his brothers and sisters—yes, even his own life—he cannot be my disciple. And anyone who does not carry his cross and follow me cannot be my disciple.... Any of you who does not give up everything he has cannot be my disciple." (Luke 14:26, 27, 33)*

These values are not reserved for a special class of disciples, while others wallow in lesser degrees of commitment. Jesus' words are the norm for the Christian young adult as well as the more seasoned believer. They describe the good steward, whose aim is to be faithful and wise in the use of all his talents.

These verses do not suggest that believers have no interests or desires of their own, or that all their interests and desires are wicked (as the counselor believed). They do emphasize unreserved commitment to the Master.

The Lord's commendation of Solomon further stresses, with great clarity, our need to subdue self-centered motivations:

"Since you have asked for this [wisdom to rule Israel faithfully] and not for long life or wealth for yourself ... I will do what you have asked. I will give you a wise and discerning heart ... Moreover, I will give you what you have not asked for—both riches and honor." (1 Kings 3:11–13)

Interests May Be Clues

Interests may be self-centered, but they can also be clues to your talents. Your interest in something may point to an area in which you could be useful, and a lack of interest may arise from a sense of personal inadequacy in that area. What interests have you followed? Have you been successful in them? Do people you respect encourage you in these pursuits?

Marc's tinkering with automobiles had its roots in his childhood years, when he would take apart any appliance he could get his hands on—the toaster, the clock radio, the lawnmower. In high school, he began working at a garage, and later he applied to an automotive training center. Today he has his own automotive business, and in the summer he volunteers to work for mission boards, at his own expense, in foreign fields. His interests were consistent with his abilities.

Rick wanted to be an architect. His interest was strong. He excelled in mechanical drawing, but his science and math aptitudes were weak, so his interests were out of sync with his capabilities. Today, he still uses his drawing abilities, but more broadly. He designs promotional materials for his church. For full-time employment, he works as a technician on computerized medical equipment. He was able to satisfy his interests in design and technical detail through both his vocational and his avocational roles. (An *avocation* is a hobby, or volunteer or part-time work, separate from one's vocation.)

Both Rick and Marc had interests that indicated how they could usefully serve God. However, they did not make their decisions solely on the basis of those interests. Imagine the disappointment and sorrow Rick might have experienced if he had sacrificed all his other talents to his interest in architecture. Instead, he realistically evaluated his abilities and chose a field that could satisfy his (modified) interests.

Fortunately, most fields offer within them a variety of positions, some of which may suit your abilities if others don't. One occupational theorist has described the job market as having fields and levels: in every occupational field, there are many levels of needed skills. In the field of health care, for example, there are a great number of different levels: nurse's aide, lab technician, orderly, secretary, medical records clerk, receptionist, computer programmer, physician's assistant, nurse (LPN and RN), general MD, specialist, surgeon—and this just scratches the surface. The same variety exists in most occupational fields: insurance, education, and the automotive industry, to name a few.

Gauging Your Interests

There are two general ways for you to examine your interests: interest inventories and occupational guides.

Interest inventories vary, but in general they ask you to mark some of your likes and dislikes about different work activities. The report you get back lists occupations which, according to your responses, might interest you. These can be helpful, but remember that they are only suggestive, not conclusive. They cannot tell you what to do. They get your attention, but then you must explore each interest area and use the other clues to your talents to help you make wise and faithful decisions. (Check with your school counselor for more information about interest inventories.)

Occupational guides are a more informal way to explore your interests. Visit your school library or career center, and look for the *Occupational Outlook Handbook*, the *Dictionary of Occupational Titles*, the *Guide for Occupational Exploration,* or other resources that organize similar occupations into groups called "clusters" (check with your school counselor for help). Read through the tables of contents of these works, scan the lists you find, and make some notes about groupings that interest you most and in which you could see yourself as a faithful steward. The Interact section for this chapter includes an exercise to help you identify some of your interest areas too.

One caution: If you have no dominant set of interests, do not let it worry you. Patty took an interest inventory; and when she got her profile, it did not help her at all. The bars on the graph of her score report were the same height in all the occupational fields, showing that her interests were similar in every area. Some students get profiles showing them to be interested in fields in which they have no interest at all.

Remember that your interests are only hints to your talents. In young adults they are usually too unstable and unsound to provide the sole basis for decision making. In contrast, your personality and aptitudes, for example, are unlikely to shift radically from month to month, or even year to year. Interests may change from week to week. Interests are just one part of the constellation of talents that God has given you.

Interests have their limitations, but they can be helpful clues to the wise investment of your talents.

Two Ways to Explore Your Interests

1. Talk to your high school counselor or adviser, and ask to register for an interest inventory that your school uses. Some popular ones are the Kuder, the Career Interest Inventory (CII), the Ohio Vocational Interest Survey, and the Strong-Campbell Interest Inventory. Be sure to review your scores in keeping with the cautions in chapter 13 about the use and misuse of interests.

2. If you do not have the opportunity to take an interest inventory, or if you wish to do a more immediate review of your interests, you may use the following exercise:

   a. First, scan the list of Worker Trait Groups (WTGs)[3] on the following pages, and circle the WTG numbers of 6 to 10 options that look interesting enough to explore further.

   b. The ability levels on the chart are typical of workers in the occupations listed. Estimate your own ability levels and compare them to those shown on the chart.

   Ability areas include:

   General: understanding instructions; able to reason; related to doing well in school
   Verbal: understanding words and ideas; able to present thoughts clearly
   Numerical: using math well
   Spatial: depth perception, visualizing geometric figures
   Form Perception: noticing differences in details of graphics or pictures
   Clerical Perception: spotting spelling, numbering, or punctuation errors, or details with objects
   Motor Coordination: eye-hand coordination
   Finger Dexterity: fingering small objects rapidly, well
   Manual Dexterity: using hands skillfully
   Eye-Hand-Foot Coordination: responding well to visual signals as in driving, operating a machine
   Color Discrimination: Sensitivity to color differences
   Occupations grouped by similar worker qualifications are called Worker Trait Groups, or WTGs.

[3] This list is adapted from Martin E.Clark, *Choosing Your Career: The Christian's Decision Manual* (Phillipsburg: Presbyterian & Reformed Publishing CO., 1989).

- Level 1 = Talents in the top third of peers
- Level 2 = Talents in the middle third of peers
- Level 3 = Talents in the lower third of peers

No.	WTG Title	General	Verbal	Numerical	Spatial	Form	Clerical	Motor	Finger	Manual	Eye/Hand/Foot	Color
01	Artistic											
01.01	Literary Arts: writing, editing, directing publications of prose, poetry, drama, for magazines, TV, publishers, etc.	1	1									
01.02	Visual Arts: drawing, painting, photography, and design for ad agencies, department stores, etc.	1-2			1	1		1-2	1-3	1-2		1
01.03	Performing Arts: drama; performing, directing, teaching for radio, TV, theater, schools, etc.	1	1									
01.04	Performing Arts: music; playing, singing, arranging, teaching groups in schools, studios, theaters, etc.	1-3	1-3			1-2	1-2	1	1	1	1	
01.05	Performing Arts: dance; composing, performing, teaching for TV, movie studios, theaters, schools, etc.	1-2			1-2			1-2			1	
01.06	Technical arts: working with graphics, handcrafts, product decoration, etc.	2			1-2	1-2		2	1-2	2		3
01.07	Amusement: entertaining in a setting such as a carnival or amusement park, etc.	2	2									
01.08	Modeling: showing how clothes and jewelry look when worn or in stores; photographers, etc.	2-3						2-3		2-3		
02	Scientific											
02.01	Physical Sciences: math, physics, chemistry; researching new materials, geology, astronomy, etc.	1	1	1	1	2	2					2
02.02	Life Sciences: study of plants and animals; solving environmental, disease problems in government hospitals, labs, etc.	1	1	1	1-2	1-2			1-2	2		2
02.03	Medical Sciences: prevention, diagnosis, treatment of disease, injury in humans and animals	1	1	1	1	1			1-2	1		2
02.04	Laboratory Technology: using equipment for chemistry, physics, or biology tests for hospitals, labs, etc.	1-2		1-2	2	1-2	2-3	2	2	2		2
03	Nature											

No.	WTG Title	General	Verbal	Numerical	Spatial	Form	Clerical	Motor	Finger	Manual	Eye/Hand/Foot	Color
03.01	Managerial Work: nature; forestry, logging, fish, animal breeding, etc.	1-2	2	2	2-3		2-3					
03.02	Genral Supervision: nature; overseeing farms, ranches, landscape nurseries, fish hatcheries, forests, etc.	2	2	2	2					2		
03.03	Animal Training and Care: for performing, helping blind, pet shops, med labs, animal shows, etc.	2-3	2-3			2-3		2-3	2-3	2	2-3	
03.04	Elemental Work: nature, using physical strength and energy, usually outside in forests, nurseries, etc.					2-3		2-3	3	2		
04	Authority											
04.01	Safety/Law Enforcement: police, fire and some businesses, mostly government hotels, stores, resorts, industries, etc.	1-2	1-2			2-3	2					
04.02	Security Services: keeping people and property safe; government hotels, stores, resorts, industries, etc.	2	2			2-3	3	2-3		2-3		
05	Mechanical											
05.01	Engineering: using sciences, math to solve construction, manufacturing, and other industry problems	1	1	1	1	1-2						
05.02	Managerial Work: mechanical; directing technical operations in industry, utility, etc.	1	1	1-2	1-2	2	2					
05.03	Engineering Technology: technical detail to apply engineering ideas such as surveying, drafting, etc.	1-2		1-2	1-2	1-2	2	1-2	1-2	2		
05.04	Air/Water Vehicle Operation: pilots for shipping and airline companies	1	1-2	1	1	1-2	2	2	2-3	2	2	
05.05	Craft Technology: skilled hand and machine work; food preparation, printing, and construction	2		2	1-2	1-2		2	2	1-2		
05.06	Systems Operation: care of equipment in heating/cooling systems, a refinery, utilities, school systems, etc.	2	2	2	2-3		2-3	2-3		2-3		
05.07	Quality Control: inspecting, checking equipment, materials, products in mines, warehouses, building sites	2		2-3	2	2				2-3		
05.08	Land Vehicle Operation: freight hauling for railroads, trucking and delivery services	2			2			2		2	2	2

No.	WTG Title	General	Verbal	Numerical	Spatial	Form	Clerical	Motor	Finger	Manual	Eye/Hand/Foot	Color
05.09	Materials Control: shipping, receiving, storing materials, keeping records/schedules, for hospitals, companies	2	2	2			2			2-3		
05.10	Equipment Operation: use of machinery for excavating, drilling, paving, mining, hoisting, etc.	2			2			2		2	2-3	
05.11	Elemental Work: mechanical; lifting, carrying materials, tools, equipment in construction				2-3	2-3		2-3		2		
06	Industrial											
06.01	Production Techology: setting up and operating production machines; supervising less skilled workers	2		2	2	2		2	2	2		
06.02	Production Work: hand and machine work learned through on-the-job training	2		2-3	2-3	2		2-3	2-3	2		
06.03	Production Control: regulating quality and quantity of products/materials; sorting, testing, recording data, etc.	2			2-3	2		2-3	2-3	2		
06.04	Elemental Work: industrial; little skill; loading/unloading machines; using simple hand tools				3	2-3		2-3	2-3	2		
07	Business Detail											
07.01	Administrative Detail: clerical work requiring special skills/knowledge for decisions in office operations	1-2	1-2	2			1-2					
07.02	Mathematical Detail: figuring, keeping records of quantities, costs in businesses, accounting firms, etc.	2	2	2			1-2					
07.03	Financial Detail: math and people skills; in jobs where money is paid, received from public, eg., banks	2	2	2			2		2-3			
07.04	Information Processing: speaking; using phones, radios in businesses, institutions, agencies	2	2	2-3			1-2	2-3				
07.05	Information Processing: compiling, reviewing, maintaining records; scheduling workers, overseeing others	2	2	2-3			1-2		2-3			
07.06	Clerical Machine Operation: use of machines that compute, sort, send, and receive data	2					1-2	1-2	2	2-3		

13

Interact

No.	WTG Title	General	Verbal	Numerical	Spatial	Form	Clerical	Motor	Finger	Manual	Eye/Hand/Foot	Color
07.07	Clerical Handling: filing, sorting, copying, routing, delivering data	2-3	2-3				2		2-3	2-3		
08	Persuasive											
08.01	Sales Technology: selling technical equipment such as industrial machinery; also insurance/mfg. reps	1-2	1-2	1-2		2	2					
08.02	General Sales: retail and wholesale stores and businesses	2	2	2			2					
08.03	Vending: peddling inexpensive items in public areas, gatherings, street corners; as in sports arenas, clubs	3	3	2-3					2-3	2-3		
09	Accommodating											
09.01	Hospitality Services: helping people feel at ease; planning social events; guides; hotels, airlines, museums	2	2				2-3					
09.02	Barbering and Beauty Services: haircuts, facials, styling	2	2		2	1-2		1	2	2		2
09.03	Passenger Services: bus, taxi, limousine, or other passenger vehicle	2		2-3	2			2		2	2	
09.04	Customer Services: services associated with commercial settings, in stores, hotels, restaurants, etc.	2-3	2-3	2-3			2-3	2-3	3	2-3		
09.05	Attendant Services: services for comfort of customers in hotels, athletic clubs, airports, etc.	2-3	2-3						3	2-3		
10	Humanitarian-Ministry Oriented											
10.01	Social Services/Christian Work: helping people through counseling, guidance	1	1	2								
10.02	Nursing and Therapy Services	1	1-2	1-2	2	2	2-3	2-3	2	2		2-3
10.03	Child and Adult Care: working in clinics, hospitals, day care, and treatment centers	2	2				2-3	2-3	2-3	2		
11	Social-Ministry-Business											
11.01	Mathematics and Statistics: computer system work with research in colleges, firms, government agencies	1	1	1	1		1					
11.02	Educational and Library Services: teaching, counseling, library work in schools, libraries, colleges	1	1	2			1-2					

No.	WTG Title	General	Verbal	Numerical	Spatial	Form	Clerical	Motor	Finger	Manual	Eye/Hand/Foot	Color
11.03	Social Research: working with groups and individuals with current social and personal problems	1	1	1-2			1-3					
11.04	Law: corporate, real estate, criminal, etc. lawyers and paralegals	1	1	1-2			2					
11.05	Business Administration: management of agency for health, counseling, education, welfare services, etc.	1	1	1-2			2					
11.06	Finance: design, control, analysis of financial information in finance department of businesses, banks	1	1	1			1-2					
11.07	Services Administration: management of agency for health, counseling, education, welfare services, etc.	1	1	2			2					
11.08	Communications: writing, editing, translating; newspapers, businesses	1	1	2			2					
11.09	Promotion: advertising, fund-raising in businesses, colleges, professional groups	1	1	1-2			2-3					
11.10	Regulations Enforcement: concerns finance, people's rights, health, safety law; mostly governmental	1-2	1-2	2	2-3	2-3	2					
11.11	Business Management: directing activities of a company or store; supervising others	1-2	1-2	2		2-3	2					
11.12	Contracts and Claims: negotiating contracts, investigating claims for insurance companies, etc.	1	1	2			2					
12	Physical Performing											
12.01	Sports: competing, coaching, officiating	2	2-3		2-3	2-3	2-3	1	1	1	1	
12.02	Physical Feats: acts of special strength or skill to entertain; circuses, theaters	2			1	2		1-2	1-2	1-2	1	

c. Estimate and compare your ability levels to the ability levels beside each occupational grouping. (Refer to your "Tested and Untested School Abilities" from Interact 12.) Mark the groups that your ability levels are most similar to.

d. Select three WTG titles in which you can envision yourself serving as a faithful and wise steward. List these titles under "Interests" in the "Professional Growth Area" segment of your CSProfile on page 174.

Worker Trait Groups of Interest:

_____

_____

_____

e. Use your selected WTG numbers and titles to refer to more occupational detail in the *Guide for Occupational Education* in your library or career center. You can also find information about these areas by looking for similar titles in the *Occupational Outlook Handbook, The Encyclopedia of Careers, The Chronicle Occupational Library,* and other library or career center resources.

chapter fourteen

Clues to Your Talents: Your Spiritual Gifts

Mel became a Christian while he was in high school. He then got involved in his local Campus Life club and saw the Lord use his influence in several other students throughout his high school years. Because Mel was not brought up in a Christian family, his parents had never really encouraged him to think about vocational, or full-time, Christian work. He was a good student and excelled in math; therefore, after graduation, he went to the University of Maryland and majored in math.

While there, Mel became a committed part of a Christian fellowship on campus. He led some small-group Bible studies, discipled other Christians, and was influential in the lives of many believers and unbelievers. When he was a junior, the pastors of his church invited him to teach and to lead some small groups in the church. At that time, as his gifts for teaching and leading became more and more apparent, Mel began to think about developing these abilities for pastoral or missions work. When he shared his interest with his pastors, they encouraged him to think about entering seminary after graduation.

Today, Mel is the senior pastor of a church in New York. He doesn't believe his math degree was a mistake. "There is no greater help to me than my math training in breaking a passage of Scripture apart and putting the sense of it back together in an understandable way. But I wasn't ready to make any decisions about ministry while I was in high school. It wasn't until college that my pastoral gifts became evident. I needed to grow first."

The Purpose of Spiritual Gifts

Spiritual gifts are specific talents, given to Christians alone, for the benefit of the church. "Now to each one the manifestation of the Spirit is given for the common good." (1 Corinthians 12:7) (In its context, *manifestation* refers to gifts that belong to members of the church.)

If you are a Christian, Scripture teaches that you have at least one spiritual gift. To "each one," Paul says, gifts are given. And you are to use the gift(s) that you have been given for the benefit of the body of Christ, the church. This is not an option. You do not need to wait for a special "calling" to use your gift. Those who serve in official ministerial positions need the counsel and recognition of godly leaders. (1 Timothy 3:1 and Acts 13:1–3) However, you are called to use whatever gift you have. Maybe you do not have the gifts to serve in a professional ministry position. Instead, your calling may be to serve in volunteer and lay positions among His people.

Some Christians, like Mel, choose to use their gifts vocationally, in full-time Christian service as teachers, pastors, missionaries, youth workers, musicians, church secretaries, and so forth. Many church and parachurch workers use their gifts avocationally (alongside their main occupation). Your gifts are part of the talent resources God has entrusted to you, and you are accountable for using them. Every Christian is called to use his or her gifts, if not vocationally, then part-time.

How to Detect Spiritual Gifts

Every major passage of Scripture that discusses the spiritual gifts (1 Corinthians 12–14; Romans 12:3–8; Ephesians 4:7–16) describes them in the context of the local church. Though many fine books have been written to encourage Christians to think about their spiritual gifts, you can discern your gifts with accuracy and confidence only through serving and interacting with other members of God's church. Are there ways in which people see you as a helpful part of your church or youth group? What is there about your work in the nursery, the children's church, or Sunday school that makes you valuable? Only through such specific, hands-on interaction with a local church or body of believers will you be able to discern and confirm your spiritual gifts.

Godly people in your church can offer valuable counsel to help you understand your gifts and how they may be most useful to Christ's church in full-time or part-time work. Like Mel when he was young, it is probably too early for the leadership in your church to make strong recommendations to you about your gifts. They will become clearer as you grow and continue to serve in the coming years, whether in college or in a vocation. God is the author of gifts, and He is not going to keep their identity from you. Through His church, He will let you know what they are, how to develop them, and when and where to use them. But you need to be part of a church body and committed to serving God's people so that the church can give you the helpful feedback you need.

What to Look For as a Young Adult

There are several passages in the New Testament that list specific spiritual gifts. Romans 12:6–8 identifies prophesying, serving, teaching, encouraging, giving, leading, and showing mercy. Other passages give more examples. 1 Peter 4:10–11, however, gives a summary of the gifts that young believers may find most helpful: "Each one should use whatever gift he has received to serve others, faithfully administering God's grace in its various forms. If anyone speaks, he should do it as one speaking the very words of

God. If anyone serves, he should do it with the strength God provides, so that in all things God may be praised through Jesus Christ...."

Speaking gifts and serving gifts make up the two broad categories into which all the New Testament gifts can fit. As a high school or college-age young adult, your involvement in your church may not have been extensive enough for you to be too specific about your gift or gifts. However, you may be able to sense the direction in which your gifts mostly lie: speaking or serving.

If you are a believer, give thought to your spiritual endowment. At this point, all you may know is that, because the Bible teaches that you are gifted, you are gifted. You may not have any idea what your specific gifts are, but it is more important that you maintain an attitude of complete submission. Commit the matter to God in prayer; commit yourself to being involved in a local fellowship of believers; seek counsel from His Word and from His people; and in time, His time, you will know well enough.

Your Spiritual Gifts

Spiritual gifts are talents that God entrusts to His people to build up the church of Christ. Christians gain an idea of what their gifts are through the experiences they have while serving among God's people. As with other talents, feedback from others is important in determining your gifts. Spiritual gift discovery is not just a private matter between you and God. All the major passages in the New Testament that talk about gifts describe the body of believers, the church, serving each other. Your awareness of your gifts will increase throughout your life as you serve among the church.

Like many young adults, you may not be deeply involved in your church right now. If you are a believer, however, you can look at even your limited service among believers to get a general idea about your more prominent gifts.

Two Broad Categories
———

1 Peter 4:10–11 sketches two broad categories of spiritual gifts: serving and speaking.

"Each one should use whatever gift he has received to serve others, faithfully administering [the New Testament word for being a steward] God's grace in its various forms. If anyone speaks, he should do it as one speaking the very words of God. If anyone serves, he should do it with the strength God provides."

Complete the Preliminary Spiritual Gift Assessment that follows. It is "preliminary" because you are doing it on your own. Write your conclusion in your CSProfile on page 174 in the segment marked "Spiritual Gift Emphasis."

This is an informal assessment. The outcomes of this do not mean that you are limited to one or another gift emphasis for the rest of your life. This is to increase your awareness of where you are now. Paul makes it clear that spiritual gifts can be cultivated and can change. (1 Corinthians 12:31)

Preliminary Spiritual Gift Assessment
———

1. Read through the following list of ministries and rate your involvement in each. Use the scale below and write the first letter of the word that best summarizes your involvement in the space to the left of each number. Use your best judgment.

Scale:
L = Little or no service in this area
S = Some involvement (i.e. more than three times a year but not regular monthly or weekly service)
R = Regular or nearly regular monthly or weekly involvement

_____1. leading Bible studies

_____2. visiting newcomers

_____3. assisting with Sunday school

_____4. leading youth meetings

_____5. being an active secretary for a group

_____6. nursing home/ jail/ children's home ministry

_____7. passing out tracts

_____8. singing before a group, leading singing

_____9. playing/ accompanying with an instrument

_____10. helping with book room/ church library

_____11. church office work: filing, typing, photocopying, computer data entry, etc.

_____12. helping with Bible clubs, vacation Bible school

_____13. helping older/ needy people of the congregation

_____14. being a good listener to people with concerns

_____15. hosting, assisting as a host(ess) to church groups

_____16. helping with maintenance of the buildings or grounds

_____17. helping with transportation needs

_____18. nursery and child care work

_____19. discipling someone

_____20. writing for church or youth publications

_____21. running a meeting

_____22. leading a discussion

_____23. tutoring someone in an area of your strength

_____24. doing art work for posters/ publications/ projects

_____25. taking charge of publicity for events

_____26. calling people to remind them of needs, programs, etc.

_____27. being a receptionist

_____28. visiting people in the community to witness

_____29. cleaning for needy people or the church

_____30. purchasing supplies for groups

_____31. sewing for needy people or projects

_____32. cooking and serving church meals

_____33. mailing/ stuffing envelopes

_____34. leading prayer meetings

_____35. writing to missionaries

_____36. organizing activities for retreats

_____37. working on a short-term missions project

_____38. Other:

_____39. Other:

2. Go back over your ratings and circle the numbers of the items you marked with **S** or **R**.

3. In the left margin next to each of your circled **S** and **R** responses, write _speak_ or _serve_. Speaking activities involve mostly speaking, and serving activities involve mostly other kinds of help. Some may involve serving and speaking equally. If so, write both words.

4. Does your involvement give you an awareness of one gift emphasis or the other? If so, copy _serving_ or _speaking_ under "Spiritual Gift Emphasis" in the "Professional Growth Area" segment of your CSProfile. If both seem to be indicated equally, copy both. If your experiences have been too limited to discern a gift emphasis, leave the space empty for now and plan to become more involved in your church.

---

part three

How to Determine the Will of God for Your Career

At the end of the movie *Star Wars*, there is a crucial scene where Luke Skywalker needs to make a perfect shot with his missile. He knows what he needs to do, but he doubts whether he has the ability to be successful.

After reading the last nine chapters, you, too, may doubt your ability to pull it off. You know what you are supposed to do—you should base your career plans on a commitment to serve God with your talents—but you don't know how to go about doing it. What are your most important talents? How can you best use them for God? How can you be sure that you are doing the right thing? How will you know?

Fortunately, as Christians, we have a surer and more realistic guide than Luke Skywalker's mystical "force." We have God's Word, given to us in the Bible, which offers commands to direct us and principles to guide us.

In addition, we have the counsel of other brothers and sisters, the ability to observe God's providential circumstances in our lives, and because of the Holy Spirit, the capacity to think about all these things and make wise life-shaping decisions.

The next four chapters will clarify the way to determine and apply God's wise plan for your life-shaping decisions.

chapter fifteen

Wisdom Is God's Will

Now Your Decisions Matter

When you were young, your parents made most of your decisions for you, but it's different now. You face dozens, perhaps hundreds, of decisions daily. Some are minor, some major: Will you gripe at your mom when she calls you in the morning? Will you talk to the people at the bus stop, or just keep to yourself? Will you laugh at the "stupid" question one of the boys asks in physics class, or empathize with him because you don't really understand either? Will you study in study hall, or will you try to get the attention of that person you've had your eye on lately? Will you work 15 or 25 hours this week? Will you use your $52.00 paycheck to buy things you "need," like that new compact disc or that designer sweater that just went on sale, or will you save your money for later? Your decisions are sometimes simple and trivial and sometimes profound and life shaping. In either case, you are now responsible for most of your decisions: the buck stops with you.

In the *Peanuts* cartoon strip, Lucy has a sign that reads, "Answers to Life's Questions, $.50. Homework Help, $5.00." As you face decisions, you will get advice from some people who, like Lucy, are willing to give it generously, even free of charge. Not all advice is bad, of course, but it is easy for people to give it when they don't have to live with the results. You, on the other hand, have to live with your choices. This chapter will help you focus on God's principles for making sound decisions in the all-important area of career planning.

Thinking in a New Dimension

You have changed in many ways since puberty. Your physical changes are perhaps the most obvious, but once your pituitary gland began kicking some of its messengers into action, your thinking abilities altered too. You can now think abstractly, idealistically, and creatively. Not only can you think about the way things are; you can also think about the way they might be, or ought to be. Developmental psychologists call this a shift from "concrete operational thinking" to "formal operational thinking." Your thinking is no longer as controlled by your senses as it was when you were a child. Then, you'd choose a nickel over a dime because the nickel looked bigger. Now your choices are affected by your ability to use reason apart from the messages of your senses. You have new, profound abilities, which have also made you newly and profoundly responsible.

Teresa was angry. She couldn't understand why her mom didn't trust her. On the morning that I saw her, the two assaulted each other with arsenals of sharp words. Teresa lost, and she was fuming: "She is so unreasonable. She doesn't trust me at all, and I haven't done anything to deserve her treating me this way. I love my mom, and I know she loves me; but why does she have to treat me like a child all the time?"

Teresa had asked her mother for permission to go to the mall after the basketball game with some girls and guys from her junior class. Her mom had two objections. First, she wasn't so sure she liked the friends Teresa would be hanging out with. Second, Teresa had to take the SAT the next morning, and she wanted her to be well rested. Teresa didn't agree. She felt she would get plenty of sleep, and she thought her friends were fine.

"Suppose you were your mother," I said to her. "Suppose you had a sixteen-year-old daughter like you. What kind of thoughts would you have that would make you respond as your mom did?"

"I wouldn't treat my daughter like that. I'd trust her to make her own decisions about friends and how long to be out."

"Perhaps, but just to think it out, what possible reasons might you have for not letting your daughter do what you've asked? Assume that you love her, as your mom loves you."

From that point on in the conversation, Teresa began to list reasons why she might have made the same kind of decision with her daughter. She began to balance the ideal of trust with the reality of a mother's need to care for a daughter who lives in an imperfect world. Teresa did not end up agreeing with her mother at every point, but she did see that her mom had solid reasons for her decisions.

Like Teresa, you have this ability to think about an ideal, to dream, and to make plans about the future. Sometimes your new ideas create tensions with parents or with friends, with a boss or co-worker, simply because you see things from different perspectives. But you can turn these problems and controversies to your advantage. They can help you to think more realistically and to reason more maturely, if you are willing to look at your own decisions and attitudes from others' perspectives. You do not have to yield to other people all the time (quite the opposite), but at least you must be able to see where they are coming from. You are thinking in a new dimension as a young adult.

Wisdom: Thinking God's Way

Proverbs was written for young adults. Solomon collected many of the sayings that his father, David, had taught him, and wrote them down for his own children to help them with their choices. He repeatedly uses the words wise or wisdom (113 times) to describe the way he wants us to think when we make decisions: "get wisdom" (Proverbs 4:5); "Wisdom is supreme; therefore get wisdom" (Proverbs 4:7); "for wisdom is more precious than rubies, and nothing you desire can compare with her" (Proverbs 8:11). Wisdom is good decision making. It is thinking about any aspect of life with God's values in mind. It asks, "How does God want me to think about this?"

God has given us all the resources we need to help us to think wisely and to know why our choices are good ones. In the next chapter, we'll look at those resources and how to use them. For now, it is important to see that God has created us to be thinkers. Sometimes Christians push their thinking into the background and substitute the idea of the Lord's "leading" or "calling" for God's plan for their decision making. Stewards that the Lord approves of must think. Their Master examines their decisions to see how wise and faithful they have been. He uses their track record as good thinkers and faithful workers to determine whether they are successful. Only then will He allow them to have greater privileges of service: 'Who then is the faithful and wise servant, whom the master has put in charge of the servants in his household?" (Matthew 24:45)

Well-meaning Christians often use spiritual but ambiguous language to describe how they made some of their important decisions. This can lead others to downplay their personal responsibility or look in wrong directions for help.

"The Lord is leading me to the University of Delaware," Trevor confidently asserted. But when I asked him how he knew this was the Lord's leading, he stumbled, looked a bit embarrassed, and said, "That's where Anne [his girlfriend] is going; and everything she's told me about it seems positive."

"I'm not sure which door the Lord is opening for me," Sheila confided. "I've been accepted at all these schools, and I don't know which to choose. My parents say it doesn't matter to them, as long as I do what the Lord wants."

Sam spoke dejectedly: "My folks want me to go to Covenant College, but I don't have any peace about it. If I go there, I may not be in the center of God's will."

Nathan was vibrant. "Everything points to Cedarville University. The money, my folks, my pastor, even the extracurriculars they offer. 1 don't know what the big deal is about deciding what to do next year. I just prayed, and God made all the circumstances work together perfectly. Cedarville, here I come!"

"I applied to four schools," Pete said. "Whichever one accepts me first is the one the Lord will be leading me to. I've put out a fleece like this before, and the Lord has helped me."

All five of these young people have put their own thought processes in the back seat. They admirably depend on the Lord, but they mistakenly substitute their relationship with Him for their own responsibility to think and choose wisely. God does lead, give peace, order circumstances, open and close doors; but He does so as we follow through on our responsibility to think, plan, evaluate, research, listen, pray, and obey. God does not want you to put your mind in neutral because you are a Christian; He wants you to think even harder.

This is true in every area of the Christian life: how to choose friends, how to approach a problem, whom to speak to about the gospel and whom to avoid, how to share the gospel, how to answer people's questions and address their concerns, and even how to eat and drink. You need to make judgments and decisions about all of life's concerns. They can be wise or foolish, thoughtful or careless, informed or ignorant, God-centered or self-centered.

Tim decided to attend Williamson Trade School. His parents could not afford a four-year college, and he wanted the carpentry skills and moral environment that this program offered. He knew several Williamson students, and he knew his grades would qualify him for admission. Because of some Bible studies in the dorms, the Christian teachers, and his ability to continue and increase his involvement in his local church, he thought that this would be the wisest course of action.

Al was in the top ten percent of his class and wanted to put all his talents at the Lord's disposal for some kind of full-time Christian vocation. He decided to get several years of concentrated, college-level Bible training; therefore, he applied to Philadelphia Biblical University. He knew that whatever direction he would pursue after college, his biblical training would be valuable. Even if he did not go directly into Christian work, he knew that many businesses would not care what his training was in. They would just want him to have successfully completed college. After hiring him, they would train him with the specialized knowlege they would want him to have.

Maureen participated in two of her church's short-term mission trips in her junior and senior years of high school. She was especially thrilled to be part of the Children's Bible School ministry during these trips. Her heart yearned for these needy, lost children. She wanted to enter a Christian college and pursue an elementary education major to prepare for cross-cultural ministry. Her pastor suggested Covenant College.

Bill had immersed himself in his computer since eighth grade. He had taken all the advanced math and physical science courses his school offered. His SATs were in the upper 1300s, and he had scholarship offers from a wide range of excellent Christian and non-Christian colleges. He had been in a Christian high school and wanted to put himself in a non-Christian college as a witness and to prevent himself from getting spiritually soft. His mother couldn't afford tuition; as a result, he chose to accept a generous scholarship to the University of Delaware.

Tim, Al, Maureen, and Bill are all thinking Christians. They sought to be faithful and wise with their opportunities and talents. They all prayed, sought counsel, considered their experiences, personalities, sexual identities, abilities, interests, and gifts. But no two of them saw exactly the same factors as important in their decision-making:

- To Tim, his practical background and parents' income (experiences) and his continued growth (personality, sexual identity, and gifts) were most important.
- To Al, his desire to serve (interests) and grow (personality and sexual identity) were strongly influenced by the counsel he had received from his youth pastor. They had visited, preached, and witnessed together (experiences) enough for the church leaders to urge Al to consider Christian work seriously.
- Maureen's experiences also were in the foreground of factors influencing her choice. The young people's response to her care and love as well as her teaching whetted her appetite for service among children in the third world.
- Finally, Bill's academic record (ability) and single-parent background (experience) were dominant features in his thinking.

All these young adults wanted to do the will of God. For each of them, this meant making wise decisions—thinking.

If you are a Christian, the Bible says that you are transformed by the renewing of your mind. You then pursue God's will by using your new Spirit-influenced, biblically centered mind. "Do not conform any longer to the pattern of this world, but be transformed by the renewing of your mind. Then you will be able to test and approve what God's will is—His good, pleasing, and perfect will." (Romans 12:2) You must think. This is the way you make decisions in areas as important as whom to marry and what kind of college to attend, and as unimportant as whether to stop at McDonald's or Burger King. Although these kinds of decisions differ enormously in their seriousness, they both require you to think wisely. Paul's urging is for you to have a mind submitted to God's purposes and open to His Word.

You are called on to use your mind in every area of life. Prayer, the counsel of others, the Holy Spirit's ministry, and circumstances are important too, but mainly as they help you apply the wisdom of God's Word to your situation. We'll look more fully at each of these in the next chapter. Here we want to examine how important thinking is for the steward.

1. Look up each passage below, and describe the situations that people are told to think and make decisions about.

    a. Proverbs 2:12–13

    _____

    _____

    _____

    b. Proverbs 4:13–15

    _____

    _____

    _____

    c. Proverbs 5:1–3

    _____

    _____

    _____

    d. Proverbs 6:6–11

    _____

    _____

    _____

e. Proverbs 6:20–26

_____

_____

_____

f. Proverbs 7:4–5

_____

_____

_____

g. Proverbs 9:7–9

_____

_____

_____

h. Proverbs 10:5

_____

_____

_____

i. Proverbs 10:9

_____

_____

_____

j. Proverbs 10:19, 32

_____

_____

_____

k. Proverbs 11:14

_____

_____

_____

l. Proverbs 11:22

_____

_____

_____

m. Proverbs 11:24–26

_____

_____

_____

n. Proverbs 13:16, 20

_____

_____

_____

o. Proverbs 13:24

_____

_____

_____

p. Proverbs 14:8

_____

_____

_____

q. Proverbs 14:15

_____

_____

_____

r. Proverbs 17:9

_____

_____

_____

s. Proverbs 19:2

_____

_____

_____

t. Proverbs 19:17

_____

_____

_____

u. Proverbs 21:5

_____

_____

_____

v. Proverbs 21:13

_____

_____

_____

w. Proverbs 22:3

_____

_____

_____

x. Proverbs 22:24–25

_____

_____

_____

y. Proverbs 23:1–2

_____

_____

_____

z. Proverbs 24:11—12

_____

_____

_____

aa. Proverbs 24:27

_____

_____

_____

bb. Proverbs 24:30–34

_____

_____

_____

cc. Proverbs 25:20

_____

_____

_____

dd. Proverbs 27:12

_____

_____

_____

ee. Proverbs 27:18

_____

_____

_____

ff. Proverbs 27:23–27

_____

_____

_____

gg. Proverbs 29:7

_____

_____

_____

hh. Proverbs 31:8–9

_____

_____

_____

ii. Proverbs 31:26–28

_____

_____

_____

2. Thinking is important to the Christian in unique ways as well as those above. Look up each of these passages and summarize how thinking is important to the believer.

   a. Matthew 7:6

_____

_____

_____

   b. Romans 6:11–13

_____

_____

_____

   c. Romans 12:1–2

_____

_____

_____

   d. 2 Corinthians 6:14–18

_____

_____

_____

e. 2 Corinthians 10:4–5

_____

_____

_____

f. Colossians 1:9–10

_____

_____

_____

g. 1 Peter 3:15

_____

_____

_____

chapter sixteen

How to Get Wisdom

Although God's Word doesn't give specific commandments about what you should do in every situation, it does offer principles that can thoroughly equip you for all your decisions. This is why the Apostle Paul encouraged the young pastor, Timothy, to put his confidence in the Scriptures as his primary tool for helping people. The Bible addresses every kind of situation and need that people face: "All Scripture is God-breathed and is useful for teaching, rebuking, correcting and training in righteousness, so that the man of God may be thoroughly equipped for every good work." (2 Timothy 3:16, 17) The Bible thoroughly equips people to make their own decisions and gives them the resources to help others. God has tailored His Word to your most significant needs. This doesn't mean that there is a command in the Bible for every decision we must make. God has given us many specific instructions that we should follow. But for most of our decisions, His Word will help us think about a wise course of action through the principles He's taught and illustrated.

Tom knows that to come home at two in the morning after promising to be home at midnight is to break God's commandment against lying. But the commandments are not as helpful when Tom has to decide which of three colleges to attend, whether to live on campus or commute, or whether or not to work for a year before going to trade school. He must think hard about these choices. However, he isn't adrift at sea. Tom can get great help from God's Word, which suggests at least four ways we can "get wisdom."

Make Wisdom a Priority

Jerry Lucas, a former pro-basketball player, wrote *The Memory Book* to help people use their powers of memory better. A key point he makes is that, to remember, you must remember that you must remember. He called it "original awareness." That is, be aware that you want to remember that person's telephone number, that appointment, or that woman's name. The same is true for wisdom: if you want to get wisdom, the first thing you need to do is remember that you want to get wisdom. You must make "getting wisdom" a priority. Solomon repeatedly urges you to desire wisdom. It isn't enough for you simply to talk about being wise, prudent, and understanding. If you truly want to be wise, you must make that desire heartfelt and insistent.

Get wisdom, get understanding; do not forget my words or swerve from them. Do not forsake wisdom, and she will protect you; love her, and she will watch over you. Wisdom is supreme; therefore get wisdom. Though it costs all you have, get understanding. Esteem her and she will exalt you; embrace her, and she will honor you. (Proverbs 4:5–8)

Blessed is the man who listens to me, watching daily at my doors, waiting at my doorway. For whoever finds me finds life and receives favor from the Lord. But whoever fails to find me harms himself; all who hate me love death. (Proverbs 8:34–36)

Go back and underline the verbs in these verses. They emphasize that you must aggressively seek wisdom: *get, find, esteem, love, embrace, do not forget, do not forsake, listen, watch, daily wait.* You must pursue wisdom constantly if you want all that wisdom promises.

A Lamp and a Light

"Your Word is a lamp to my feet and a light for my path." (Psalm 119:105) "The unfolding of your Words gives light; it gives understanding to the simple." (Psalm 119:130)

Light illumines. It dispels shadows; it reveals obstacles and opportunities. God's Word is a lamp for the faithful steward. As His Word "unfolds" in our hearts, it provides the light of knowledge that can assist in the most difficult of career decisions. "Should I put college on hold and get a job?" "Should I enter military service?" "Should I go to community college?"

In order to understand the principles of God's Word, we will have to give up thinking that all of life is like instant oatmeal, instant pudding, or instant coffee. Instead, we must meditate regularly upon God's Word. This will take time, but only in doing so can we become "like a tree planted by streams of water, which yields its fruit in season and whose leaf does not wither." (Psalm 1:3) If we do meditate on God's Word "day and night," God promises that whatever we do will "prosper." (Psalm 1:2–3) One teacher has called meditation the "stomach" of the Christian life. Like the stomach, meditation takes chunks of Scripture and breaks them down into spiritually nutritional forms that improve our spiritual health and help us to apply God's wisdom to all of life's situations.

Solomon says that, in order to get such wisdom, we must "look for it as for silver and search for it as for hidden treasure…." (Proverbs 2:4) Many of us are so accustomed to gratifying our desires instantly, that we become easily discouraged or frustrated in our personal devotions. We hold a priceless jewel in our hands, encrusted with dust, and, after a few casual attempts to brush off the dust, we throw it aside, assuming that it isn't worth the trouble or that there is not a jewel in there after all.

It is more difficult to think about how biblical principles apply to situations and decisions we face than to wait passively for God to open doors for us or lead us without the mental hard work of careful thought.

But God has already led us, in His Word, to His Word. The door is always open to study Scripture diligently to gain the principles necessary to be a wise and faithful steward.

Plans Fail for Lack of Counsel

Each of us naturally longs to act independently and make our own decisions, whether great or small. This longing is fine, so long as we do not seek complete and total independence—a kind of personal anarchy. We need to remember that God has put others (parents, teachers, pastors, counselors, peers, etc.) in our lives to make us part of an interrelated and interdependent world.

God did not create man to be independent of other people or of God Himself. He said that it was not good for Adam to be alone (Genesis 2:18), so He created Eve to complete him. Male and female naturally depend on each other. Our interdependence goes beyond the marriage union, though, to include our relationships with others in the church. The New Testament describes the community of believers by a metaphor: the body of Christ. First Corinthians 12, Ephesians 4, and Romans 12 all employ this metaphor to describe our inter-relationships.

> *Now the body is not made up of one part but of many. If the foot should say, "Because I am not a hand, I do not belong to the body," it would not for that reason cease to be part of the body.... If the whole body were an eye, where would the sense of hearing be? If the whole body were an ear, where would the sense of smell be? But in fact God has arranged the parts in the body, every one of them, just as He wanted them to be. If they were all one part, where would the body be? As it is, there are many parts, but one body. (1 Corinthians 12:14–20)*

What is true for men and women, and for the church, is true for every one of us, Christian and non-Christian. Solomon makes it clear in Proverbs that we must recognize our interdependence, not just husband to wife, Christian to Christian, but person to person. Man is a social being, placed in a social context of relationships on which we can draw for wise counsel and guidance. "Plans fail for lack of counsel, but with many advisers they succeed." (Proverbs 15:22) "For lack of guidance a nation fails, but many advisers make victory sure." (Proverbs 11:14) "Do you see a man wise in his own eyes? There is more hope for a fool than for him." (Proverbs 26:12)

As we showed earlier (chapter 15), advice can be cheap. But if you are wise in whom you select for advice, you can make prudent, practical, and, what is most important, biblically sound decisions. Good counselors, those with a professional title or just friends, can open your eyes to how biblical principles may apply to certain situations. Further, they may stimulate your own meditation on God's Word to find even greater implications. Their advice may not be specific or even profound, but they can often give you helpful comments and ideas to keep in mind as you plan.

Ted applied to the state university as a biology major. His high school counselor considered his academic record and suggested that he think about another course of action. He told Ted that his grades and SATs were not as high as the state university requires for the biology or pre-physical therapy major. The counselor recommended that Ted apply with an undeclared major, prove himself, and then reapply to the major after he showed he could handle college science and math.

Ted thought this was too slow a route to his goal, so he stuck with his original plan. In February, Ted received his disappointing letter of non-acceptance. He went to his counselor for help, a little more humble this time. The counselor called the admissions director who had signed Ted's letter. He agreed that Ted would have had a better chance of acceptance as an undeclared major and said that if he sent a letter requesting that change, they would be happy to reconsider him. Ted sent the letter and, in September, started at the university as an undeclared major. At the end of his freshman year, he reapplied to the pre-physical therapy major and was accepted.

Counselors are not the Lord. They are not all-knowing and should not be listened to just because they are counselors, but often they have good reasons for their suggestions. Ted would have been wiser if he had thought about his counselor's ideas and agreed or disagreed on the basis of sound reason and not just according to a timetable he had set. "The wisdom of the prudent is to give thought to their ways, but the folly of fools is deception." (Proverbs 14:8, see also Proverbs 14:15)

Tony came into his youth pastor's study looking as if all the cares of the world were on his shoulders. "I don't know what to do," he said. "My folks are pushing me to make a decision about what to do after graduation, and I don't have any idea at all."

"What kind of thinking have you done, Tony?" his pastor asked.

"Well, I've prayed about it," he quickly replied. "But God hasn't answered yet."

"But what kind of thinking have you done? How has your praying helped you think more clearly or completely?" his pastor persisted.

Tony sat bewildered. "What do you mean?" he asked, "I have prayed about whether to go to college next year or to work for my dad, but I still don't know which the Lord wants me to do."

Tony's attitude is common for some Christian young people. Praying is necessary but only one of many things we need to do when we approach our decision making. When Christ tells us to pray "Give us this day our daily bread" (Matthew 6:11), should we assume that we have nothing more to do than pray in order to be fed? Similarly, while it is necessary for us to pray about our decisions, we cannot expect God miraculously to deliver the answers to us. We must think.

Kelly had a wide variety of options. She had offers from colleges because of her basketball, academic, and student leadership involvement. She also had to decide whether to go away to school (and away from her family, with whom she was very close), or to commute. She said that as she prayed during her second semester, she began to consider the importance of staying home and remaining involved in her church, a factor she had not considered to be as serious at first. As she prayed, God made her thoughts, and her decision, clearer.

Prayer is not a two-way conversation. The writer of Hebrews tells us that "In the past God spoke to our forefathers through the prophets at many times and in various ways, but in these last days He has spoken to us by His Son...." (Hebrews 1:1–2) Such miraculous communication continued through to the times of the apostles, but God no longer speaks in this direct fashion, not since His Word was completed. In it we can find all the direct communication we need to live a life that is holy and pleasing to God. (John 17:17; 2 Timothy 3:16–17)

Nowhere in all the New Testament letters to believers is there a command or encouragement to look to God for some miraculous guidance apart from His written Word.

This is not to say that God has not occasionally, mysteriously impressed certain people with a sense that they ought to make a particular decision about something. But using these impressions for decision making is not encouraged in the New Testament as God's usual pattern for His people. The careful, prayerful, counseled thinking with principles of His Word in mind is God's method for making our life-shaping decisions. (Colossians 1:9; Psalm 119:120; Proverbs 30:5,6; 2 Timothy 3:17; 2 Peter 1:3)

Prayer is important. As a steward, you need to pray in order to make wise decisions, but prayer is not a hotline to God through which He answers all your questions. It is His means for you to "present your requests to God." (Philippians 4:6) It is His way for you to ask for wisdom in any difficult situation. "If any of you lacks wisdom, he should ask God, who gives generously to all without finding fault, and it will be given to him." (James 1:5) But even here, James is not teaching that God will reveal something directly to a believer. The wisdom he writes about, for which we are to pray, is the godly character the Lord wants His people to exhibit in times of trial. (James 3:17)

You need to make wise choices. Prayer is a critical part of coming to wise conclusions, not because God sends voices, visions, or dreams to you, or because He makes you feel a certain way, but because He helps you make wise choices. He sharpens your mind and spirit to interpret your situation realistically, to evaluate counsel honestly and humbly, and to consider biblical principles accurately and submissively.

Prayer is not an option for the steward; it is a necessity. But neither is it a shortcut to get answers to hard questions and decisions. In the same way that a personal time of meditation on the Scriptures is indispensable for spiritual nurture, so prayer is indispensable. If meditation is like eating, prayer is like breathing. Both equip you to think spiritually so that you can make faithful stewardship decisions.

No Bricks Without Straw

The Egyptian Pharaoh forced the Israelites to make bricks without straw when he was angry about Moses' request to let God's people go from slavery. The straw helped the clay and mud to hold together and produce strong bricks. The Israelites had to go find their own straw and were held accountable for making the same quota of bricks—a nearly impossible task.

We have no such vindictive Master. He loads us with talents and will hold us accountable to invest them wisely, but He doesn't leave us to scrape around for our own bits and pieces of ideas about how to do that. He also gives us the necessary guidance to make sound plans. He directs us to get wisdom, to meditate on His Word, to refer to the counsel of others, and to speak directly to Him. The result is a plan for faithful and wise career stewardship that will please Him, bring Him glory, and provide us greater opportunities to serve Him and to enjoy satisfying happiness.

To get wisdom, a young adult must cultivate certain attitudes and use the resources God has placed in his or her life.

1. After reading these passages, describe the attitudes that are implied as requirements for becoming a wise person.

    a. Proverbs 4:5–8

    _____

    _____

    _____

    b. Proverbs 8:34–36

    _____

    _____

    _____

    c. Proverbs 14:8

    _____

    _____

    _____

    d. Proverbs 14:15

    _____

    _____

    _____

2. After reading these passages, identify other important considerations that you need to include in your thinking in order to make wise choices.

a. Psalm 119:105

_____

_____

b. Psalm 119:130

_____

_____

c. Timothy 3:16–17

_____

_____

d. 2 Peter 1:3

_____

_____

e. Proverbs 11:14

_____

_____

f. Proverbs 15:22

_____

_____

g. Proverbs 26:12

_____

_____

chapter seventeen

You Don't Need a Crystal Ball to Make Wise Choices

Stacy lay in her sleeping bag beside her best friend, Brenda. They had started this adventure five days ago—hiking, rafting, and climbing—but the sheer face of a cliff and the rushing, churning water of the river were nothing compared to the ominous shadows dancing on the tent walls. "Was that a man's arm? A bear's head?" she whispered, as her imagination ran wild. She didn't remember when she dozed off, but when the morning began to break, she awoke, slid out of her sleeping bag, and crawled over to the tent flap. She pulled the zipper up a couple inches and peered out at the campsite. Looking up, she saw the leaves on the trees and the clothes she had hung to dry, and realized the moonlight had made them seem more ominous than they were. Her sigh of relief woke Brenda.

Back in civilization, there were ominous shadows of a different type. I answered the phone to hear a voice that was more frantic than usual: "Dr. Horne, this is Mrs. Ramford. I need your help with my son, Sean. I have tried to help him but he simply has no idea what he wants to do with his life. Can you meet with him and try to help him?"

I was puzzled. "Sure, I'll be glad to meet with your son." While I listened to her explain the seriousness of Sean's situation, I searched my mind to recall who Sean was, but I couldn't remember. "Mrs. Ramford," I began apologetically, "I'm sorry. I thought I knew all the upperclassmen, but for some reason I can't picture Sean. What grade is he in?"

"Oh," she said a little more meekly, "he's in ninth grade, in Mr. Samuelson's homeroom."

Mrs. Ramford thought Sean's future was in jeopardy since, as a high school freshman, he didn't have his career plans mapped out. He hadn't selected the job he wanted for the rest of his life, and he hadn't chosen the college or major he'd need to get the job. To his mother, these unmade decisions were ominous shadows flickering on the wall of her son's future. The shadows caused Mrs. Ramford to fear that Sean was in danger, when it was her own irrational fears that presented the real threat. Such shadows, unfortunately, affect how we plan our careers. Unanswered questions can pressure us to make foolish choices that can have long-term effects on our career planning.

"You Gotta Know Now"

Mrs. Ramford's attitude is a good example of the "you gotta know now" syndrome. Parents and friends often give young adults the impression that they almost need to be prophets, that they need to see the future clearly in order to make plans today. After all, before young men and women can put their career plan together, don't they need to know what they "want to do with their life," "what they are cut out for," or "what God wants them to do"?

How much of ourselves and our future do we have to know before we put our plans together? James gives us God's answer:

> Now listen, you who say, "Today or tomorrow we will go to this or that city, spend a year there, carry on business and make money." Why, you do not even know what will happen tomorrow. What is your life? You are a mist that appears for a little while and then vanishes. Instead, you ought to say, "If it is the Lord's will, we will live and do this or that." (James 4:13–15)

Not only is it unnecessary for you to know your earthly future, it is impossible. You can and should think about what is wise for your future plans, but you need to view those plans with a humility that first says, "If it is the Lord's will, then…." Often the attitude "you gotta know now" rests unwisely on the notion that career planning is a once-in-a-lifetime opportunity—we do it while in high school or college, and for the rest of our lives we have to live with the course we have charted. The problem is that such an attitude rests on a distorted view of the work world, and more importantly misreads God's expectations for faithful and wise stewards.

Quite often your plans for the future will change, whether you want them to or not. Marty, for example, was a lab technician who became intrigued with some of the computerized equipment he was using that was regularly breaking down. He looked into continuing his education in computer technology. He enrolled in an evening and summer program and, after a year and a half, got a job as a technician with a distributor of medical equipment. Planned changes like this are "par for the course" today.

But workers are also forced to expand their abilities by a fluctuating job market. Jay, for example, had been the manager of a retail computer store that had to close. With short notice, he was looking for a new job. He already had some contracting experience, and he had earned a reputation as a hard worker. Before long, he got a job as foreman of a painting crew for a small contractor.

Such midcourse changes are not at all unusual—they are the norm. In today's job market, high school graduates can expect to have between eight and twelve different employers, and perhaps as many as four completely different occupations throughout their work lives. One study estimates the average length of time at a job has decreased to 3.6 years. The job market will always be unpredictable; and even though the government has attempted to forecast future trends, they can arrive at only rough guesses.

God expects us to use our minds to think about our alternatives in all situations, at all times. "The wisdom of the prudent is to give thought to their ways." (Proverbs 14:8) "A prudent man sees danger and takes refuge, but the simple keep going and suffer for it." (Proverbs 22:3) The prudent person will reflect and change directions if he thinks it will help him to be a wise and faithful steward. A good career choice this year, whether it be a school or a job, may need to be altered next year. You may find your finances strained, or you may have a new, demanding family situation. Your college curriculum may shift, or you may not be able to keep your grades up in your major. Any of a thousand unpredictable circumstances that are completely beyond your control may intervene and cause you to rethink your plans. According to Solomon, only a fool perseveres down a path regardless of the consequences.

Though the details of your future are unpredictable and though your career will probably take some unplanned turns, if you are committed to being a faithful steward, you can still plan with confidence. You are bound to make mistakes in judgment along the way. Mistakes are natural to our imperfect and limited humanity.

Nevertheless, "in all things God works for the good of those who love him." (Romans 8:28) This is not just a pious saying that Paul offers. On the contrary, it helps us to refocus our sights on what is most important: loving God. While our plans may not succeed in the world's eyes, we will have achieved the greatest success possible if we love God and are committed to being His faithful stewards. Through the prophet Isaiah, God urges His people to maintain such confidence, despite difficulties: "Fear not, for I have redeemed you; I have summoned you by name; you are mine. When you pass through the waters, I will be with you; and when you pass through the rivers, they will not sweep over you. When you walk through the fire, you will not be burned; the flames will not set you ablaze." (Isaiah 43:1–2)

This does not mean that a Christian will never encounter difficulties—quite the opposite. If you are a Christian, you will pass through deep waters and walk through fiery flames. Job taught us, "Man born of woman is of few days and full of trouble." (Job 14:1) But God asserts that the rivers won't overwhelm and the fire won't consume His faithful stewards even if their career plans appear to have gone awry.

You do not need to be anxious because you do not know what you will be doing in ten years or because you may have to change your plans. You do not need to know with certainty anything about your occupational future to put solid plans together now. What you need is a view of yourself as a steward and an idea of the talents that God has entrusted to you. Be faithful with these, and the Master will cause your little knowledge to go a long way. "Whoever can be trusted with very little can also be trusted with much. "(Luke 16:10) "You have been faithful with a few things; I will put you in charge of many things." (Matthew 25:23)

You Don't Need a Crystal Ball to Make Wise Choices

"You Gotta Know Now!"

1. According to James 4:13–15, how much of your future do you need to know before you can make wise and faithful decisions?

Read James 4.13–15.

    a. How much certainty about how a job would work out was necessary in order for those early Christians to be faithful?

_____

_____

_____

    b. What attitude(s) does James encourage in this passage?

_____

_____

_____

2. Before they could begin working as faithful stewards, how much certainty about their occupational futures was necessary for the Christians in the following passages?

  a. Ephesians 6:5–8

     ❑ Very Certain   ❑ Certain   ❑ Somewhat Certain   ❑ Unnecessary

  b. Colossians 3:22–24

     ❑ Very Certain   ❑ Certain   ❑ Somewhat Certain   ❑ Unnecessary

  c. 1 Thessalonians 4:11, 12

     ❑ Very Certain   ❑ Certain   ❑ Somewhat Certain   ❑ Unnecessary

  d. 2 Thessalonians 3:11, 12

     ❑ Very Certain   ❑ Certain   ❑ Somewhat Certain   ❑ Unnecessary

e. 1 Timothy 5:8

❏ Very Certain   ❏ Certain   ❏ Somewhat Certain   ❏ Unnecessary

3. From each of the following passages, what attitudes and knowledge are most important for the Christian steward?

a. Ephesians 6:5–8

_____

_____

b. Colossians 3:22–24

_____

_____

c. 1 Thessalonians 4:11–12

_____

_____

d. 2 Thessalonians 3:11,12

_____

_____

e. 1 Timothy 5:8

_____

_____

"Once-in-a-Lifetime"—A Paralyzing Notion!

Is it true that if we don't make all the right decisions at the beginning of our career planning we are doomed to a terrible future? Do you get only one chance to do it right!?

4. After reading each passage, explain the changes that each person or group had to accept as part of God's plan for them—difficult as some of the changes may have been.

     a.   Hebrews 10:33, 34 (the reaction of the Hebrew Christians to unexpected changes caused by persecution)

_____

_____

_____

     b.   Genesis 50:15–21 (Joseph reviewing his brothers' jealous actions toward him when he was younger)

_____

_____

_____

     c.   Judges 6:11–7:25 (God raising a ruler in Israel)

_____

_____

_____

     d.   Ruth 1:19–2:3; 4:13 (Ruth's departure from her homeland in Moab and later marriage to Boaz)

_____

_____

_____

e.   1 Samuel 9 (a change in Saul's occupation)

_____

_____

_____

f.   1 Samuel 16 (David's role change)

_____

_____

_____

g.   Amos 7:14–15 (his job)

_____

_____

_____

h.   Matthew 4:18–22; 9:9 (disciples who changed occupations)

_____

_____

_____

5.   Now go back to each situation above and put yourself in the place of the person or persons facing change. What feelings do you think you might have had if you had been the person in each situation? What negative reactions might you have been tempted to have if you had acted on these feelings?

_____

_____

_____

_____

6. Each of these people or groups experienced occupational change of one sort or another. How would you complete the following statement?

Their changes were not failures or caused by mistakes, but were ...

_____

_____

_____

7. Think about adults you know who have undergone occupational changes. (Please use no names.) What reactions have you witnessed? What kinds of thoughts and feelings may have contributed to those reactions? What biblical principles might have helped those people if they had meditated on them?

_____

_____

_____

_____

_____

_____

_____

_____

_____

_____

_____

_____

_____

_____

_____

_____

_____

chapter eighteen

Christian Service: Which Stewards Do It?

The theme of the church's missionary conference for this year was "The Church Planting the Church." After the conference, Tim felt guilty because he was not planning to go to a Christian college to prepare for a career as a missionary, planting churches. None of the speakers limited missions or Christian service to evangelizing and beginning churches, but that was the emphasis Tim came away with. He had developed a narrow idea of what it meant to serve the Lord with his life.

Is Christian service limited to what pastors and missionaries do? Is it something a young man or woman is prepared to do only if he or she has Bible or Christian college training? Is it primarily reserved for highly gifted people? Are full-time jobs in ministry fields of greater value to God than occupations such as teaching karate, doing auto body work, illustrating for a periodical, working as a lab technician, or being a manufacturer's representative?

All Work Has Dignity

Work has dignity and value because it is part of God's plan for all people. God created humans as workers before sin even entered the human race. "The Lord God took the man and put him in the Garden of Eden to work it and take care of it." (Genesis 2:15) God gave humans a worker identity the day He created them. "God blessed them and said to them, 'Be fruitful and increase in number; fill the earth and subdue it. Rule over the fish of the sea and the birds of the air and over every living creature that moves on the ground.' " (Genesis 1:28) As we work with attitudes and values of faithful stewards, we fulfill God's command to us to rule over the creation.

After Adam and Eve sinned, God said toil and pain would be added to work as part of the curse they brought upon themselves: "Cursed is the ground because of you; through painful toil you will eat of it all the days of your life. It will produce thorns and thistles for you.... By the sweat of your brow you will eat your food." (Genesis 3:17–19) Then, to make sure that people would not underestimate its importance, God made work a part of His moral law—the Ten Commandments. "Six days you shall labor and do all your work, but the seventh day is a Sabbath to the Lord your God. On it you shall not do any work." (Exodus 20:9–10) He did this to remind us of the value of work and to make us face squarely a responsibility that we might now prefer to avoid because of our sin nature. God put boundaries on both sides of work in His commandments. To guard against laziness and neglect, He said people were to work six days. To guard against making work an idol, He said people were to work *only* six days. The seventh belongs to Him.

In the New Testament, we find these commandments to work echoed by the apostles. Paul commanded that "if a man will not work, he shall not eat" (2 Thessalonians 3:10) and "if anyone does not provide for his relatives, and especially for his immediate family, he has denied the faith and is worse than an unbeliever" (1 Timothy 5:8). Likewise, believers are "not to give up meeting together" on the Lord's day and other occasions. (Hebrews 10:25) Work is important, but it must not be made an idol.

All Work Is God's Platform

All of life is a platform from which to glorify God. "Whether you eat or drink or whatever you do, do it all for the glory of God." (1 Corinthians 10:31) If we are to do the mundane activities of eating and drinking consciously to God's glory, then surely God includes our work roles in the wide net of "whatever you do." Workers who glorified God in biblical history include shepherds, contractors, farmers, political rulers, tentmakers, workers with textiles, physicians, teachers, lawyers, engineers, masons, artists, musicians, civil servants, soldiers, businessmen and women, managers, fishermen, writers, public speakers, horticultural workers, bodyguards, stone cutters, masons, poets, secretaries, pastors, missionaries, evangelists, and many more.

Some of these workers were in the background, supporting the frontline workers and leaders in God's kingdom; some were on the front line. While certain vocations are more influential than others, God assigns no superior value or dignity to one vocation over another. He is looking for faithful stewards in every area. He entrusts us all with different talents and expects us all to use them as wisely as possible to accomplish His purposes. God illustrates this with the "body" metaphor in several New Testament passages. All His people, without respect to their position, sex, race, or socioeconomic status, are important for His work.

"Now the body is not made up of one part but of many. If the foot should say, 'Because I am not a hand, I do not belong to the body,' it would not for that reason cease to be part of the body.... But in fact God has arranged the parts in the body, every one of them, just as he wanted them to be.... But God has combined the members of the body and has given greater honor to parts that lacked it, so that there should be no division in the body, but that its parts should have equal concern for each other." (1 Corinthians 12:12–26)

We can think of the importance of all types of workers from another perspective: the unity of the Christian's life. There is no "sacred" and "secular" separation in a Christian's life. Everyone is to live his or her life as a "living sacrifice." (Romans 12:2) All believers are "salt" (Matthew 5:13), "light" (Matthew 5:14), "witnesses" (Acts 1:8), "ambassadors" (2 Corinthians 5:20), "disciples" (Matthew 28:19–20), "soldiers" (Ephesians 6:10–18), and "stewards." (Matthew 25:14–30)

It is true that some workers, such as pastors, translators, church planters, Christian school teachers, and missionaries are on the front lines battling to advance the Kingdom of Christ, while others such as mechanics, public school teachers, homemakers, insurance agents—most of us, as in any battle formation—are in important supporting positions.

However, nobody is insignificant. Whether one can give 40, 60, or 80 hours a week for Christian service in full-time ministry or 40, 60, or 80 hours of Christian service in the world's professional fields, God's stewards are at work for His glory. All Christians are in full-time Christian service.

Christian Service Is Not an Option

While Tim's guilt at the Missionary Conference may have been false, his sense of obligation to use his life to serve Christ was not. He was right to start asking himself how God wanted him to obey the Great Commission to "go and make disciples of all nations." (Matthew 28:19)

All Christians must obey this command. No Christians are on the spiritual welfare roles because of Christian service unemployment. The last words of Jesus to His disciples in Acts 1:8 were a review of their, and our, identity: "you will be my witnesses."

Twice in the Gospel of John, Jesus summarized the life of service He had for all His followers. "As the Father has sent Me, I am sending you;" (John 20:21) and, "As you sent Me into the world, I have sent them into the world." (John 17:18)

All stewards must plan to develop and invest their talents with Christ's Great Commission in mind. Jesus didn't say we were to go and make disciples after we achieve the basics of the great American dream: graduate from college, have a job, get married, have a home, two children, two cars, and an IRA.

This means faithful young adult Christians must make plans that include sharpening themselves for Christ's service. They are, as we have seen, "salt," "light," "witnesses," "ambassadors," and "soldiers."

Jesus tells His disciples to pray that "the Lord of the harvest" will "send out workers into his harvest field." (Matthew 9:38) Frontline workers are needed in today's harvest field: young men and women whose love for Christ motivates them to serve Him in vocational ministries that aim directly to extend the kingdom of God.

Not everyone, of course, should serve in this way. It is not the wisest and most faithful use of every young person's talents to engage in vocational Christian service. And not all believers meet the stiff qualifications for ministry in 1 Timothy 3 and Titus 1. But all Christian young adults should consider this kind of work because of (1) Christ's love: "for Christ's love compels us … that those who live should no longer live for themselves but for him who died for them" (2 Corinthians 4:14, 15); (2) Christ's command: "therefore go and make disciples of all nations" (Matthew 28:19); and (3) the world's need: "the harvest is plentiful but the workers are few." (Matthew 9:37)

Christian Service Often Evolves

Tim, the confused young man at the opening of this chapter, went on to a state university. He pursued his business education, and after graduation he worked in, then managed, an insurance office in eastern Pennsylvania for four years.

In time, however, his quiet but clear testimony of faith in Christ opened the opportunity to begin a Bible study among work associates. For two years, he and his wife led the study and had the privilege of leading a few people to faith in Christ. With the support of his wife and the encouragement of his church leaders, he decided to begin training for pastoral ministry. This was not a desire that he had while in high school. It developed and was fanned into a flame through his involvement in his local church and a Bible study.

Tim was in Christian service in his work role in the office, in his home as a husband, in his Bible study, and later in his church ministry as a pastor. All four roles were equally vital Christian service.

Tim chose his post–high school education thoughtfully. Even today he does not regret his university education and business experience. If you talk to him, he gives credit to these early experiences for much of his ability to manage the many aspects of his ministry and to apply God's Word practically.

We are engaged in Christian service in every work role at every stage of our lives as Christians. God's intent is to use us to make an eternal difference in the lives of people in the world—with or without a Christian ministry label.

The Great Privilege of Vocational Christian Service

While all work has dignity and worth before God, there are privileges that accompany the decision to use our talents in a more frontline role. Of course, there are often drawbacks, such as a low salary (usually), little regard from the world for the worth of our work, and the likelihood of becoming the greater target for Satan's attacks in his war against God's kingdom. But the opportunity to use the major part of our work life to advance Christ's rule is a privilege second to none, and it carries the promise of great blessing too. Following are two of the greatest benefits.

Enjoyment of the Lord

David expressed the delight he had in serving when he said, "Better is one day in your courts than a thousand elsewhere; I would rather be a doorkeeper in the house of my God than dwell in the tents of the wicked." (Psalm 84:10)

David's experience does not imply that vocational Christian work is of greater value than other occupations. Rather, the more energy we can devote directly to Christian ministry, the greater will be our opportunity to enjoy the delights of communion with Him in His courts.

Another psalmist expressed the deep longing of his (and every believer's) heart to meet with God. "As the deer pants for streams of water, so my soul pants for you, O God. My soul thirsts for God, for the living God." (Psalm 42:1–2) Then he asks where this meeting can take place. "When can I go and meet with God?" (Psalm 42:2) The Christian always has access to God's presence, of course. But vocational Christian work gives the believer the privilege of being in the presence of her living, loving Father as a major part of her work role—fellowshipping with Him, talking to Him, and enjoying Him.

Extraordinary Opportunity to Extend the Kingdom of God

Every believer helps to establish Christ's kingdom by serving Him. But vocational Christian workers have the privilege of exerting more of their energy to do it.

The Apostle Paul teaches that all believers build either faithfully or foolishly in their service, but all believers build. Christian workers who have their full time to devote to ministry have the further privilege of faithfully building more.

> *By the grace God has given me, I laid a foundation as an expert builder, and some-one else is building on it. But each one [Christian worker] should be careful how he builds. For no one can lay any foundation other than the one already laid, which is Jesus Christ. If any man builds on this foundation using gold, silver, costly stones, wood, hay or straw, his work will be shown for what it is, because the Day will bring it to light. It will be revealed with fire, and the fire will test the quality of each man's work. If what he has built survives, he will receive his reward. If it is burned up, he will suffer loss; he himself will be saved, but only as one escaping through the flames. (1 Corinthians 3:10–15)*

Amazingly, in addition to giving Christians the opportunity to build in ways that make a difference for eternity, Paul says here that God examines the works of all builders and graciously rewards their faithful service. More soberly, though, He also holds His people accountable for unfaithful building.

Jesus also described the benefits of service:

> *"I tell you the truth," Jesus replied, "no one who has left home or brothers or sis-ters or mother or father or children or fields for me and the gospel will fail to re-ceive a hundred times as much in this present age (homes, brothers, sisters, mothers, children and fields—and with them, persecutions) and in the age to come, eternal life." (Mark 10:29–30)*

No one can outgive God, and He takes notice of every kind of service we render.

Gene and Gail decided to go to the Philippines as dorm parents in a school for missionary kids. "Not only has it been a great privilege for Gail and me to help support the work of church-planting missionaries, but we believe our own children have benefited from being in a non-Western culture."

Andy has chosen to devote three months a year to meeting mechanical and equipment needs for some of the evangelism and relief efforts that a Latin American mission has developed.

Ted uses his math skills in a Christian school to help parents provide a nurturing atmosphere for their children. Gina has become a secretary for a faith mission. Grace uses her communications training from Temple University to help a mission, a Christian school, and other Christian works by designing literature, video, and other media presentations for out-reach and fund-raising.

How each of these people will personally benefit from their choices, only eternity will tell. But the promise of God is that no one outgives Him. As Jim Elliot, a missionary martyred in Ecuador in 1956, wrote to explain his choice of vocational Christian work, "He is no fool who gives what he cannot keep to gain what he cannot lose."

Your Life Can Make a "World of Difference"

One counselor challenged a group of young adults to think about spending some portion of their lives in a non-Western or third world country. "Why be a teacher in a country where, if you don't take a job teaching, someone else will? Why be a mechanic in a country where, if you don't take a job in that field, someone else will? Why not be a teacher, mechanic, computer technician, lab technician, physician, nurse, secretary, mason, contractor, or accountant in a country where; if you don't do it, it won't get done? Why not use your life to sow seeds in a field that gets little attention but one where the Lord of the harvest wants His laborers to go?" "The harvest is plentiful but the workers are few. Ask the Lord of the harvest, therefore, to send out workers into his harvest field." (Matthew 9:37, 38)

You can make a difference! Faithful and wise career stewardship by all believers will bring the Master's praises and rewards. Faithful and wise career stewardship by vocational Christian workers includes greater costs than other Christians usually face, but it also offers greater privileges than others usually enjoy. "Well done, good and faithful servant! You have been faithful with a few things; I will put you in charge of many things. Come and share your Master's happiness." (Matthew 25:23)

Christian Service: Which Stewards Do It?

1. Are some kinds of work Christians do for employment more spiritual than others? (Think in terms of occupations like machinist, Christian counselor, physician, engineer, salesman, teacher, and pastor—rather than things like bartending, managing a casino, or selling illegal drugs.) Look up each passage below and determine whether God has His favorite occupations for His people. What kind of work does God value as the most important or as His "highest calling"?

1 Corinthians 7:21–23

_____

_____

Colossians 3:22–24

_____

_____

1 Corinthians 10:31

_____

_____

2. What ought to be the Christian's major goals in his or her work?

2 Thessalonians 3:8

_____

_____

2 Thessalonians 3:9

_____

_____

2 Thessalonians 3:10

_____

_____

1 Timothy 5:8

_____

_____

1 Timothy 6:1

_____

_____

Ephesians 4:28

_____

_____

1 Thessalonians 4:11–12

_____

_____

Titus 2:10

_____

_____

3. What obligation do believers have to find gainful employment? What if they do not? (2 Thessalonians 3:10, 11)

_____

_____

4. How is the believer described who does not provide for his family? (1 Timothy 5:8)

_____

_____

5. What should the work and attitudes of Christians be like, whether or not they like their work?

Ephesians 6:5

_____

_____

Colossians 3:22–23

_____

_____

Ephesians 6:7

_____

_____

Ephesians 6:6

_____

_____

2 Thessalonians 3:8; Ecclesiastes 9:10

_____

_____

2 Thessalonians 3:11–12

_____

_____

Titus 2:9

_____

_____

Titus 2:10

Ephesians 5:16

Colossians 3:17

---

6. What kind of relationship should Christian workers have with their employers whether they like their employers or not?

Ephesians 6:5; Colossians 3:22

Ephesians 6:6–8; Colossians 3:23

Ephesians 6:6

---

1 Timothy 6:1; 1 Peter 2:18

---

7. Consider the following ways Scripture describes the Christian, and mark whether God is encouraging service on a personal level or a professional level:

a. Matthew 5:13   ❏ Personal   ❏ Professional

b. Matthew 5:14   ❏ Personal   ❏ Professional

c. Matthew 25:19–23   ❏ Personal   ❏ Professional

d. Matthew 28:19–20   ❏ Personal   ❏ Professional

e. Acts 1:8   ❏ Personal   ❏ Professional

f. 1 Peter 2:9–12   ❏ Personal   ❏ Professional

g. 2 Corinthians 5:20   ❏ Personal   ❏ Professional

h. 1 Corinthians1:26–29   ❏ Personal   ❏ Professional

part four

Where the Rubber Meets the Road

If you have worked your way through *Life-Shaping Decisions*, you are more than ready to take some practical post–high school planning action.

The following three chapters may help you do that. The first illustrates how the parts fit together for the wise servant. The second, "A Tale of (Travelers to) Two Cities," is a modern parable about the two most common approaches to college decision making. The third, and also the last chapter in this book, sketches the way you can use what you've learned about yourself in the process of making a college choice. Much more practical detail about this last process can be found in the author's companion book *Walking Through the College Planning Process, which is also published by ACSI.*

chapter nineteen *part four*

Illustration of Career Stewardship

A Biblical Case History

He was only 17 years old. It looked as if he had everything going for him. His family was wealthy. He lived on a large estate, and his parents loved him deeply, perhaps too deeply. But he had a problem. His eleven brothers were jealous of him. His dad loved him the most and let the brothers know it. Their jealousy grew into resentment and finally into violence.

Joseph lived about 4,000 years ago, yet his career followed a series of twists and turns that forced him to face many of the same decisions that young adults face today. Some of his crises were the result of decisions he made. Others came because of circumstances beyond his control.

Joseph had at least two dreams that gave him confidence that God would be with him throughout his life. Both dreams showed him rising to a position of honor and authority over his family and even over much of the world. He shared the first dream with his brothers and then, not too wisely, he shared the second also. His brothers' jealousies were kindled; and within a short time, they beat him up, threw him into a pit, and began to plot his murder. Instead of killing him, however, they decided to sell him as a slave to a caravan of merchants en route to Egypt.

When Joseph was a teenager, his career did not look very bright. He had used bad judgment (in telling his dreams to his brothers), he had bad references (his brothers and parents), and he was at one time a slave with no freedom to choose the direction for his life—he had no options. On the plus side, he did have the assurance, through his visions, that God was somehow going to use him and cause his life to prosper. When he was in the pit and on the caravan, that assurance must not have seemed very realistic. But he was willing to hold onto it by faith in the Lord.

In Egypt, a government official named Potiphar bought Joseph and was soon impressed with his faithfulness and responsibility. He promoted Joseph to be the CEO (chief executive officer) of all his affairs so that "with Joseph in charge, he did not concern himself with anything except the food he ate." (Genesis 39:6) Joseph's integrity and wise decision making led Potiphar to place great confidence in him. It also led Joseph to a much wider range of career opportunities and personal freedoms.

But there was a surprising downturn in Joseph's life, and the cause was outside Joseph's control. Potiphar's wife unjustly accused Joseph of making sexual advances toward her. Potiphar threw Joseph into prison. Again, the hopes of his teenage visions must have been nearly dashed. How could God be glorified through Joseph's reputation as an immoral, untrustworthy steward?

But even Joseph's prison cell was part of God's plan; it was "the place where the king's prisoners were confined." (Genesis 39:20) Joseph's behavior in prison does not suggest that he knew the specifics of God's plan for him, but it does suggest that he was holding onto God's promise. Joseph sought to be faithful in his new role, and in time his persistence bore fruit. The "warden put Joseph in charge … and he was made responsible for all that was done there." (Genesis 39:22) Again, the Lord used Joseph's faithful and wise judgment to move him along a career path that placed him in a pivotal position in God's plan, not only for his future, but also for the future of Israel.

The next two chapters (Genesis 40 and 41) summarize a series of events in which Joseph's special ability to interpret dreams came to Pharaoh's attention. The Lord had positioned Joseph to win Pharaoh's favor; and eventually Joseph advanced to become the second most powerful person in the kingdom. With this new position came virtually unlimited freedom.

In every circumstance—under Potiphar, in prison, under Pharaoh—Joseph seems to have been aware that he was a steward, and he strove to be a wise and faithful one. His motivation and his mental energy emerged from his commitment to follow God's plan for his life whether he knew the details or not. When his brothers came face to face with Joseph later in life, while he was second in command in Egypt, they feared for their lives. Brutal vengeance was in Joseph's power, but he forgave them: "Don't be afraid.…You intended to harm me, but God intended it for good to accomplish what is now being done, the saving of many lives." (Genesis 50:19, 20)

Today, believers who engage in career planning can have the same confidence, as long as their primary goal is faithful stewardship to God. Their confidence does not come from dreams and visions like Joseph's. But God assures us in His Word that He will use His stewards in significant ways to accomplish His eternal purposes. Like Joseph, we must exercise human responsibility and trust in divine sovereignty. God tells us that we can do both with the assurance that in all things God works for the good of those who love him (Romans 8:28), and that we have been created in Christ to do good works (Ephesians 2:10), that is, to serve the living God (Hebrews 9:14). Whatever you do, work at it with all your heart, as working for the Lord, not for men, since you know that you will receive an inheritance from the Lord as a reward. It is the Lord Christ you are serving. (Colossians 3:23–24)

chapter twenty

A Tale of (Travelers to) Two Cities

They were unusual cities. Like other cities, they had their own citizens, their own governments, their own ethical systems, and their own cultural values. But "cities" may not actually be the best word for them, since they both occupied the same time and space. The people in both cities had each other for neighbors, worked in the same businesses and industries, enjoyed some of the same entertainment, endured the same social and economic ills, and enjoyed the same benefits. Thus there was some overlap.

But the citizens of each city were really living in two different worlds. The citizens of the city of Shalom[1] tried to live and work productively with God's values in mind. The city fathers were strong believers. They sought to encourage the citizens to think and act in harmony with the truth. They urged the citizens to live for others, to serve the needy, to advance in their professional roles, to influence their neighbors for Christ, to model God's goodness to others, and to enjoy the spiritual, material, and social benefits that overflow from a life of faithfulness.

The citizens of the other city, Success,[2] were commonly nice people who lived with order in their lives. They were often kind neighbors, productive professionals, and civic-minded citizens. But their values and goals were radically different,[3] so their lives differed more or less seriously from the lives of their Shalom neighbors.

Success's citizens pursued educational advancement, material abundance, professional development, and the moral freedom to live as they pleased, without reference to anyone else. Commonly seen and heard in the city were slogans like "Be yourself" "Do your own thing" "Do what you need to do," and "Feel good about yourself." The people's self-centered, self-indulgent lifestyles spun off social evils that they usually tried to keep out of sight.

The poorer sections of the town, for example, grew worse at the expense of big business's sports, gambling, and adult entertainment industries. The city managed to keep hidden the thousands who contracted STDs, the tenement buildings, and the halfway houses. The abortion and pornography industries flourished because of moral "freedom" and "progressive" interpretations of the first amendment. The school system was like a war zone in which risk of violence, the use of drugs, and the dissemination of "politically correct" worldviews crippled the morally responsible behavior of many.

When it came to promoting their cities, the citizens of Success were, on the whole, far more aggressive and skillful. Many celebrities in Success endorsed its superiority, its creative billboard ads, its lively and varied entertainment options, and its many popular causes. In short, Success appeared to middle-class suburbanites to be both a respectable and a fun place to live.

Shalom was much quieter in its methods of promotion, usually depending on word-of-mouth advertising. Some of its citizens did advance to political office, business management, and other positions of esteem, and a number used their more visible platform to speak boldly about their city.

Both cities wanted to attract high school students as future citizens, including those at Ambition[4] Christian High School, the largest Christian high school in the state. ACHS graduates were attractive to the leaders in both Shalom and Success, and both tried to attract ACHS students. They each sent their view books and catalogs to the students' homes, had others phone them personally, and flooded them with mail inviting them to travel to their city. But there the similarity ended.

The route to Shalom was hedged on both sides by mysterious hi-tech lenses, all the way from high school to the city itself. Students who looked through the lenses viewed the world around them from God's perspective. The route to Success was advertised as having no restricting, oppressing hedges like those in Shalom, with its "traditionalists from a bygone era." Travelers on this route felt "liberated."

Because of their Christian commitment, virtually all the parents of ACHS hoped their sons and daughters would end up settling down in Shalom after their travels. No one questioned the wisdom of making Shalom the ultimate destination, but there were different ideas about the best way to get there. Some were guided by sound thinking—a process called "Guided by Thinking," or GT for short. The others were guided by the way they felt, or the impressions they had of what they saw—a process called "Guided by Feelings," or GF.

Some GT parents and students thought the best route was the one that led directly to Shalom. "It's clear what we must do," they reasoned. "If we want our young adults to live in Shalom, have values that reflect those of its Ruler, put their talents to good use, and cultivate godly goals[5] and motives, there is only one right road. It makes sense for the students to travel on the road that lets them see their world through God's lenses." These thinkers made their decision after serious reflection about their children's goals and maturity.

Other GT parents and students chose the road to Success with the intention of using its resources to build their lives God's way. "After all," they reasoned, "God is the author of everything true and useful. To be professionally respected and to reach out effectively to others, our students ought to take this route." These travelers were thinking about their options in light of their students' ultimate destination and the impact they might have.[6] Their parents assessed their own children's maturity, strengths, and weaknesses. They were confident about their children's ability to carry and use their own portable biblical lens. They were aware of the temptations along the Success route, but still they concluded that it offered the wisest setting, the "best" route.

Still other travelers made decisions by the GF process. They thought most about how they felt about the road, the rules of the road, the rest areas, the food, and other comfort-level criteria. Generally the GF parents who encouraged their son or daughter to take the route to Success wanted them to take advantage of its wares and then exit toward Shalom when they got close to the city. They knew that a direct route to Shalom was available, but they felt that its tolls were generally higher and that available financial aid was usually scarcer than on the Success route. They also felt that the Shalom route was not as well kept up and had fewer rest stops, less-skilled mechanics, ill-equipped hospitality centers, and poorer scenery.

GF travelers had heard of Success's dangers. They were not naïve. Their city fathers warned of them on the Lord's Day, and the parents had seen many of them firsthand, though they were not fully aware of such pitfalls as the raiding gangs, the deceptive mechanics, and the distracting and misleading billboards. Anyway, they thought their sons and daughters would travel the route to Success but turn toward Shalom after three or four years, thus enjoying the best of both worlds. On the route to Success, they would move along a smoother, more attractive road, and they would develop a résumé more appealing to the people of Success if they were interviewed for a job by one of them.[7]

ACHS parents and leaders knew that wise choices do not just happen; they have to be nurtured. To promote its mission of educating students who will serve God and impact the world through biblical thought and action, the school provided Next-Step Advising Services to its students. The goal of Next-Step was to help students think carefully about how to plan their travel route for their professional lives. ACHS wanted to give parents the support of knowledgeable professionals, to help them nurture their young adult children toward faithful, independent Christian adulthood. The Next-Step staff's charge was to help students move toward Shalom—using the route that was wisest for them.

Next-Step Advisors began to urge potential travelers to think seriously about their options. The Advisors developed print and video materials, planned seminars, made available extensive published and Internet reference resources, and even met with parents and their sons and daughters in private interviews to help them think about their options. The school's help encouraged many parents but offended some.

The Advisors were sounding serious cautions for all travelers, but they drew stark contrasts between the two cities and their corresponding routes. They affirmed that the routes were intentionally constructed, maintained, resurfaced, and promoted to lead naturally to their appointed cities.

Travelers would take routes that were like the cities they led to, either Christian or anti-Christian. The allegiance of Success's citizens was to gods of their own making, and they were hostile[8] toward the true God, His Son, and His city of Shalom. These people could be pleasant to live and work with, but in reality they were enemies[9] of the true God and His purposes. "He who is not with me is against me, and he who does not gather with me, scatters."[10]

The citizens of Success and most of the travelers on its road were living in a fantasy world. Many of them were intelligent, law-abiding, respectable friends, and neighbors, but they adopted values, motives, and goals that were out of touch with the reality of life as God had created it. They had imaginary "sand-based" security,[11] a fictitious sense of ethics and life's priorities,[12] finite and illusory goals,[13] a distorted interpretation of the world and life,[14] and natural spiritual blindness.[15] Fantasy world living to this extreme was the norm for Success's citizens.

The Advisors pointed out the two different worlds their travelers would soon encounter. They were describing the routes and their cities by the statements of Scripture. They were not criticizing those former ACHS students who were on the road to Success, but they were urging caution and alertness. They appealed to all students not to be GF travelers—especially if they chose the road to Success. They needed to think! The routes were not neutral. Both taught. Both influenced. And both were designed to do so.

Some GT parents and students would take the road to Shalom. They would use its lenses along the way, and they would mature through the experience. Some would take the road to Success, use lenses they took along, detour at the appropriate place, and end up in Shalom. The critical difference between those who matured through their travels and those who were subverted or who became complacent through theirs, on either route, was not which road they were on. It was their interest in, skills with, and use of biblical lenses to assess the values and goals that were modeled and taught along the way. It did not matter whether the travelers used lenses installed along the route or those they had taken with them. Yet, after their training at ACHS, their long familiarity with Shalom, and their frequent interaction with the City Fathers, few students seemed to use the biblical lenses thoughtfully. Many seemed unaware of the need to do so.

Increasingly, the teachers at ACHS observed that large numbers of their students lacked mature, GT levels of discernment. This motivated them to equip students with God's lenses and the competency to use them.

Likewise, the Advisors were not neutral about the best option for most travelers. Success published a number of periodicals to help travelers determine the "BEST ROUTES." But only one road promoted God's values without apology. Only one serviced its travelers with honesty and accuracy. Ultimately, while the Success route had some strong features and some wonderful people, only the Shalom route was designed to prepare people to view life from God's perspective.

The Next-Step Advisors considered their job well done if they could stimulate GT travelers, regardless of the road the students chose. Sadly, to the Advisors' more than occasional disappointment, many students were GF travelers and became enticed by the surface attractions of the routes to Shalom and Success. GF travelers on the road to Success belonged to the statistical 50 to 80 percent of Christian students[16] who started on that road and never turned to Shalom. GF travelers on the road to Shalom were easily enticed into complacency.[17] They gradually slid into assuming that their Christianity was intended to make them feel good rather than to equip them for spiritual warfare. Both of these GF traveler types would be likely to break the hearts of their parents and of the Christian workers who loved them and labored on their behalf.

But there's another side to this story. A significant number of students, with their parents' support, chose wisely and thoughtfully. They were the GT Travelers. Some took the road to Shalom; others, the road to Success. Those who matured most began their trip with discernment, understood who they were and what the world was, and were committed to fulfill God's purpose for their lives. Parents, teachers, and advisors enjoyed the deep satisfaction of seeing them graduate and make choices guided by biblical thinking. They knew these young people were on the path to Shalom. They knew these were the faithful stewards of their talents whom God would use to change the world. They knew this was the route to advance the Kingdom of God and that even the gates of Hell would not be able to prevent them from fulfilling their mission.

Test yourself!

Are you a GF traveler or a GT traveler?

1. Are you making your decisions about colleges that are best for you primarily from college-published literature or from a "best" college guide?

2. Have you visited but not interviewed professors to determine the worldview emphasis of a college or department?

3. Do you consider the negative or positive opinions of your peers as major data on which to base your decisions?

4. Are you inclined to think of non-Christian colleges as spiritually neutral, not friendly to your Christian values but not seriously antagonistic to them either?

5. Do you think of a degree from the "right" college, or a "top" college, or a "selective" college as a requirement for future job security and success?

6. Have you been unwilling to examine both Christian and non-Christian colleges to determine what will best support you to be all that God wants you to be?

7. Have you made up your mind at the start that you will or will not go to one kind of college or another?

If you answer yes to any of these questions, you may be making decisions as a GF traveler rather than a GT traveler. Yes answers may indicate that worldview issues are not of prime importance in your decision making. Other factors may be more important to you.

Endnotes

1 *Shalom* is the Hebrew word representing personal wholeness, spiritual and physical prosperity, and peace to those who live with a commitment to the knowledge and fear of the Lord.

2 *Success* is used here as a status typically measured by wealth, position, power, and/or the esteem of others.

3 Contemporary philosophers, theologians, and apologists (Charles Colson, R. C. Sproul, Josh McDowell) as well as earlier ones (St. Augustine, John Calvin, Abraham Kuyper) have elaborated on this contrast with figures such as the "city of God" and the "city of man," and the concepts of "naturalism" and "tolerance." There is no neutrality.

4 Ambition is not always bad. It can be a godly quality when it is controlled by godly motives. See Romans 15:20 and 1 Thessalonians 4:11.

5 Proverbs 22:6, "Train a child in the way he should go and when he is old he will not turn from it." One modern Christian leader has said of this verse, "It doesn't say 'train up a child in the way he should NOT go and when he is old he will not turn from the way he should go.'"

6 Proverbs 21:22, "A wise man attacks the city of the mighty and pulls down the stronghold in which they trust." To be most effective, GT travelers on the road to Success reasoned, "It's wise for me to master the world's perspective and training in my area of study. I can put a support system together to help me keep the spiritual and worldview balance that is so critical for being faithful to the Lord. I'll have to do that since I know I won't find that kind of support from the people who designed this road." See also
1 Corinthians 9:19–23.

7 Typically, only the rarer, more prestige-conscious firm cares much about the route by which one travels. At best, the name of the route opens the door for an interview. Once a candidate arrives and opens his mouth, he is judged by his appearance and how he presents himself. (See *The Very Quick Job Search*, 2d ed., Indianapolis: Jist Publishing, 1996.)

8 Romans 8:7, "... the sinful mind is hostile to God. It does not submit to God's law, nor can it do so." See also John 3:19, 20; 15:19, 20.

9 Colossians 1:21, "Once you were alienated from God and were enemies in your minds because of your evil behavior."

10 Luke 11:23.

11 Matthew 7:26, "... everyone who hears these sayings of mine and does not put them into practice is like a foolish man who built his house on sand."

12   Proverbs 10:12, "There is a way that seems right to a man, but in the end it leads to death." See also James 3:14–17.

13   Matthew 6:19, "Do not store up for yourselves treasures on earth, where moth and rust destroy and where thieves break in and steal."

14   Proverbs 1:7, "The fear of the Lord is the beginning of knowledge, but fools despise wisdom and discipline." See also Proverbs 9:10.

15   1 Corinthians 2:14, "The man without the Spirit does not accept the things that come from the Spirit of God, for they are foolishness to him, and he cannot understand them, because they are spiritually discerned." See also John 9:41 and Ephesians 2:1–3.

16   These data, 70 to 80 percent, are quoted from two different broadcasts by James Dobson, who cited Young Life as the source. Summit Ministries uses a 50 percent figure, gained through the research of one of their writers.

17   Josh McDowell and others point out that research demonstrates that the values of Christian college students are often not significantly different from those of students in non-Christian colleges. The choice of a Christian college does not guarantee that the student will graduate with a Christian worldview.

Turn Your Findings Into a Wise, Life-Shaping College Decision

The director of admissions at the University of California, Santa Cruz, has written, "Avoid the 'designer-label' trap. Prestige and quality are not always found in the same institution. Look for the elements that will most directly support who you are as a student."

Not all colleges will support who you are. This is especially true if you are a Christian young adult interested in developing your talents to fulfill God's agenda. In fact, many college mission statements express the goal of shaping you into the image that their humanistic philosophy dictates. Even some Christian colleges have blunted their edge as instruments for helping young adults develop as world-changers. Many sincerely present themselves as having a moral and evangelical posture while allowing their academic courses to be taught by people who do not subscribe to the integrity of Scripture or its foundational truths. It has been said that we may fall in if we lean too far over to speak to the modern world.

Ask Yourself the Most Critical Question

Now that you have given more thought to your talents, the most critical question you can ask to assess whether it is wise or unwise to attend a particular college is the "Best Support" question: What is the program that will *best support* me to be the whole person God has created me to be?

This question takes all your talents into account. It helps you keep your career stewardship identity and motives intact. And it encourages you to think carefully about God's will.

Two Levels of Questions with Which to Investigate

Students should explore colleges on two levels to answer the Best Support question. Stage I questions are the first level and are the easiest to answer. Stage I questions ask about the college's size, distance from home, cost, variety of majors, beauty of the campus, average high school GPA or SAT/ACT scores of entering freshmen, dining facilities, faculty-student ratios, study abroad options, clubs, dorm size, campus rules, and scores of other items. All these areas are important to explore, but this information may be found in catalogs, other literature printed by the school, or a simple visit and tour of the campus. While Stage I information is important, in five years much of it is not going to matter. The impact of other areas, however, will remain with you for the rest of your life.

Stage II questions get to the second and more serious level of information necessary for a wise choice. Stage II questions separate the "prudent" from the "simple" [naïve]. (Proverbs 22:3 warns us about being simple: "A prudent man sees danger and takes refuge, but the simple [naive] keep going and suffer for it.") Stage II questions will help you to assess how well the college will support you with its values and worldview.

Two Worldviews to Detect with Stage II Questions

No college faculty member or department is neutral. All encourage students to view life, values, goals, problems, solutions, and needs from one point of view or another. Charles Colson asserts that there are basically just two perspectives: naturalism and biblical Christianity. Jesus declared that "he who is not with me is against me, and he who does not gather with me, scatters." (Luke 11:23) Every college nurses one of these two views, consciously or unconsciously. Stage II questions will help you discern the nature and strength of a professor's or department's worldview.

The Stage II Questions

"The fear of the Lord is the beginning of knowledge." (Proverbs 1:7) Any discipline that you hope to master must be understood from God's perspective if it is to equip you to be a faithful and wise steward with your talents. Sadly, many students unknowingly choose colleges that promote an agenda of success, fulfillment, wealth, influence, and their version of security. These are the appeals that seduced the "wicked and lazy" servant in the parable of the talents in Matthew 25:14–30.

You need to evaluate every college or university in terms of whether it will help you with the goals you believe God wants you to pursue. If the program you can put together at a particular Christian or non-Christian school is the "best support" for you to become all that God intends you to be, then pursue it. If not, pass it by—regardless of its prestige, Christian label, right "feeling," beautiful campus, or scholarship offers.

Stage II questions get at the heart of the institution's values. It does not take many of these, but they do need to be asked of the right people: professors—usually not admissions personnel. Following are some samples:

Stage II Questions to Ask Christian College/University Professors

1. Are all members of your faculty committed to the inerrancy of Scripture? Who does not have a clear statement of commitment to the trustworthiness of Scripture in all areas? (Consider

especially the psychology, religion, sociology, and education departments.)

2. Are all your faculty committed to teaching their subject from God's perspective? Do your faculty believe in the sufficiency of Scripture? (This is different from number 1. Some are committed to Scripture but don't think about or know how to approach their subject from God's perspective.) How is the Bible used in this department?

3. How are the faculty in this department supervised to see that they are teaching with a commitment to Christian perspectives on their subject? (The most honest education will be one in which you are taught to understand and evaluate the world's perspectives from God's perspectives.)

4. What writing have your faculty members done (published or unpublished) that may help me to understand their presuppositions (i.e., their approach to knowledge and truth)?

5. What means does the school use to keep a sense of God's mission (i.e., His purpose for men and women in the world) before students? How would the goals of my professional training here differ from those of a state university? Who am I urged to be working for? How does the college do this Christ-centered urging?

Stage II Questions to Ask Non-Christian College/University Professors

1. I am approaching life from a Christian perspective. Will I find professors in my major field tolerant of, or antagonistic to, my convictions?

2. When I am invited to express my opinion, will I have the freedom to respectfully express my Christian perspective without being academically penalized? (Some colleges consider it their mission to shape students according to their humanistic model. In some such cases, earnest Christians are not welcome. This is often in the values-laden fields of psychology and sociology. The Christian marches to the beat of a different drummer, and these educators know it and often do not like it.)

3. Are there faculty members in this department (my major field) at the university who are evangelical Christians? Who are they? How could I get in touch with them?

Where Can I Find the Answers to My Questions?

Common Resources for Stage I Answers
- Acquire and read *The College Handbook, College Cost Book, Index of Majors* (published by the College Board).
- Acquire and read *Peterson's Guides (to Four-Year Colleges, to Christian Colleges,* etc.).
- Access and explore computer databases such as *Guidance Information System (GIS); EXPAN; CollegeView.*
- College catalogs, view books, brochures, and pamphlets.

Common Ways to Get Stage II Answers
- Interview college department faculty member(s), asking Stage II questions.
- Hold informal interviews with students in the library, dorms, dining hall, and classes of major courses that interest you.
- Read the current college newspaper.
- Talk to alumni and friends who attend or have recently attended the college.
- Read published materials by college faculty that reveal their philosophical and religious bias.

Your Career Stewardship Profile

The diagram on page 174 will help you keep in mind the wide range of talents God has entrusted to you as you think about your options for further education.

1. If you have not already done so, fill in the "Professional Growth" and "Personal Growth" spaces with a summary of data about yourself from Interacts 8–14.

2. Review these things with your school counselor, pastor or youth paster, parents, and other trusted adults. Ask these people what options for further study they would advise you to explore.

3. Research these options and begin gathering Stage I and Stage II data. You may want to use the book *Walking Through the College Planning Process* (ACSI, 2001), which will lead you step by step through a wise, specific, biblically principled decision-making process.

Finally, complete the third segment of your CSProfile. Record your thoughts and those of your counselor and parents about the program that might be wisest for you to pursue after graduation.

MY CAREER STEWARDSHIP PROFILE

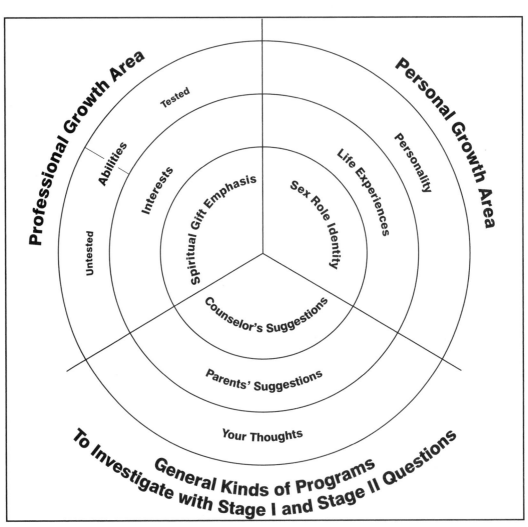

From your CSProfile above, copy the "General Kinds of Programs" that you believe you would be wise to explore:

_____

_____

_____

_____

_____